THE CANDELÁRIA MASSACRE

THE CANDELÁRIA MASSACRE

HOW WAGNER DOS SANTOS SURVIVED
THE STREET CHILDREN'S KILLING
THAT SHOOK BRAZIL

Julia Rochester

First published in 2008 by Vision,
a division of Satin Publications Ltd
101 Southwark Street
London SE1 0JF
UK
info@visionpaperbacks.co.uk
www.visionpaperbacks.co.uk
Publisher: Sheena Dewan

A catalogue record for this book is available from the British Library.

ISBN-13: 978-1-905745-26-5

2 4 6 8 10 9 7 5 3 1

Cover photo: Paulo Makita/A Tribuna
Cover design by OK?design
Text design by Matrix
Printed and bound in the UK by JH Haynes & Co Ltd, Sparkford

For Scott

CONTENTS

CONTENTS

Author's Note

AT THE END of 1994, I began work with Amnesty International's Brazil Research Team in London. One of the cases I was asked to work on was that of a young man called Wagner dos Santos. He was a key witness in the case against a number of policemen who had been accused of carrying out a massacre of street children outside Rio de Janeiro's Candelária Church in 1993. Wagner had survived two murder attempts and had just been sent to Geneva for his safety. His tenacity fascinated me, and for several years I followed from afar the various twists and turns in his story with mounting incredulity. But it was not until 2004, long after I had left Amnesty, that I met Wagner in person and asked if I might write his biography. He said yes.

The resulting book is based mainly on interviews with a number of key figures whose lives were touched by the Candelária massacre, including Wagner himself. Unless referenced otherwise, quotes are from interviews that I recorded in London, Switzerland and Rio de Janeiro between 2005 and 2007. It is a complicated story, involving a large number of people, and inevitably there are some omissions. I have attempted to fill in any gaps from contemporary newspaper articles, legal documents and Amnesty International archives. Other secondary sources, including books and documentaries which discuss the case, are listed in a short bibliography at the end of this book.

23 July 1993

WAGNER WOKE UP and lifted his head. He was lying on tarmac. To his left lay Gambazinho. Wagner knew instinctively that he was dead. To his other side lay Paulo. Wagner slowly pushed himself to his feet. He touched each of his friends just to make sure that they were not alive. They lay on the road. Blood had pooled around their heads and the thin orange light from a street lamp gave it a dull sheen. Black patches stained their clothes. Wagner had no idea where he was. He was dimly aware of low trees and a wide road. The street lights seemed to guide him towards a brighter light in the distance, one that suggested the presence of people. He allowed himself to be drawn towards it. He gave no thought to the possibility of passing cars, but simply kept going in the direction of the light. He understood that Paulo and Gambazinho were dead and that he himself had been shot in the face. There was a strange sensation in his head – a ringing sound. As he walked, he became aware that he had also been shot in the chest.

The light turned out to be a petrol station. The attendant saw a large black man covered in blood staggering towards him. He would later explain to the press that it was not the first time this had happened – it went with the job. 'No!' He called out to Wagner. 'You can't fall here. No! What have you done?'

But Wagner was falling. There was nothing he could do to stop himself. It was as though the ground was being twisted from under his feet. Everything gave way. He lay next to the petrol pump under the harsh strip lighting, and faces began to assemble around him. A siren came closer and closer, became louder and louder, and stopped. There was a face close to his own. A voice told him to turn his head to one side so that he did not choke on his own blood. He understood that this person was trying to help him. There was another siren, more people. He was being lifted. The voice, the one that was trying to help him, said, 'Get him to a hospital. Treat him well.'

In the ambulance the radio crackled. Voices broke in and out of the airwaves. One of the voices was shouting, 'They're killing everyone at Candelária! They're terrorising the city!' The words took on no meaning to him at the time. They blended in with the rest of the noise: the running of the engine, the siren, the voices of the paramedics and his own breathing – a thin liquid foaming breathing that required his concentration. It was surprising how little pain he felt. What he felt most was cold; his whole body felt cold.

It was not until he arrived in the hospital and was lying parked on a stretcher in the corridor that he remembered the radio message about Candelária, and then only because lying next to him on another stretcher, with part of his face blown away, was the person whose name the police had been shouting before they had pushed Wagner into the car. It was the Candelária kids' leader: Come-Gato.

PART I

It Happened

1

The New Democracy

WAGNER DOS SANTOS should have died on 23 July 1993. It was not the first time that he had been close to death and it would not be the last. But his not dying at the age of twenty-two was the defining feature of his life. His near-deaths followed him wherever he went, little ghosts of his former selves. He credited his survival to God, who was a real, quiet presence to him, but he did not make a fuss about that, and if people preferred to assign it to fate or the spirits, well, then each to his own. 'Some-one had to survive to tell the story,' he said. 'Justice makes itself felt one way or another.'

In 1993, Brazil was only a few years into a new democratic era. The twenty-one-year-long military regime had, in 1985, given way peacefully to a civilian government which had drafted an optimistic new constitution. Congress had recently impeached Fernando Collor de Melo, who had become Brazil's first popularly-elected president in 1989, and while the corruption which led to the impeachment had been dispiriting, the impeachment itself demonstrated that Congress had risen to the occasion. There was still hope that the democratic process would begin to address the huge social inequalities in a country that was blessed with enormous wealth yet blighted by the poverty of a vast sector of its black, indigenous and mixed-race population.

Although the structure of the state had altered, the structure of its law enforcement apparatus had not. The streets continued to be policed by the *Polícia Militar*, military police who operated according to a rigid military code, living in barracks and training like soldiers. They retained the language of combat, thinking of themselves as acting in opposition to an enemy. During military rule this enemy had been 'political subversives', but by the mid-1990s the enemy had become the population itself. Crime had escalated and the white rich feared the dark poor, especially in cities like Rio de Janeiro, where the *favelas* – the shanty towns – were associated with drug trafficking. The job of the Military Police was the containment of what was seen as a criminal class, and policing of the *favelas*, home to a third of Rio's population, was conducted almost exclusively in the form of armed incursions leading to shoot-outs with drug traffickers.

One very visible symptom of the social divide was the homeless population in Rio's city centre, which included large numbers of street kids who made a living from prostitution and petty crime. Extermination groups made up of off-duty military police, often commissioned by shop owners or hoteliers, sought to 'control' the nuisance of street kids by killing them and dumping their bodies in ones and twos on the edges of the city, where only the poor would notice. The Candelária massacre was one such attempt at 'control', but it did not go unnoticed.

The Church of Our Lady of the Candelária was at the centre of everything, right in the middle of the financial district, within ten minutes' walk from the courts, the museums, the Legislative Assembly and the naval district. It was a landmark just off Rio's busiest shopping street, the Avenida Rio Branco. It was also one of Rio's most important cultural icons, a tourist destination, and it held political significance as the site of pro-democracy demonstrations and trade union rallies. Not least, it was a powerful religious symbol, and the murder of children on a church forecourt was a profound shock to the city.

Wagner was not a street kid and many people said that he 'was in the wrong place at the wrong time', which suggested, unintentionally, that the eight boys who did die that night were not. Their fate was only to be expected. Their faces, voices and personalities quickly receded to the edge of the story. One of them lay in the morgue waiting for someone to find out his real name so that he might be buried. No one ever did, and he was buried anyway.

It was a very sad story, but Wagner did not like to be sad. He chased away his ghosts with music. His love was *pagode* – slow, traditional samba. He thought out loud in little snatches of song and carried music everywhere he went. He always had spare batteries in his pocket for his Walkman. 'Without music,' he said, 'a Brazilian is dead.'

The night before the Candelária massacre the street kids sang and danced into the night on the swirling black-and-white cobbles of the church forecourt, and Wagner, whose fate was so briefly and accidentally intertwined with theirs, drummed along, standing, as he often did, slightly apart from the group. They sang *Sarapatel*, jumping up and down to the beat, shouting out the words:

> *Quem é? ... Quem é? ...*
> *Quem go-sta de co-mer sa-ra-pa-tel?*

On the night of 23 July 1993 there were around sixty-four children living next to Candelária Church, most of them under the age of twelve, and no one in authority was accountable for them.

2

Wagner dos Santos

MANY OF WAGNER'S memories came and went as though clouds drifted across them. Everyone involved in the Candelária case had trouble with chronology – no two people could reproduce the same sequence of events. After all, they were being asked to remember events which had taken place thirteen years ago, and which had been very traumatic at the time. Weeks might stretch into months, months into years. Years might telescope into a moment. Compounding this for Wagner were the two bullets that remained in his head. One had shattered in his neck, and the other was moving about somewhere behind his right ear.

Perhaps his first complete memory was from when he was about six. His father was out of the picture, either in jail or off with another woman or Wagner's mother had left him again after a particularly severe beating.

Wagner had good memories of his mother. He could not remember her ever hitting him. They were living out on the edge of Rio de Janeiro, in one of the flat, dusty *favelas* off the roaring Avenida Brasil, the eight-lane highway that took the traffic west out of the city. They were collecting cardboard to sell. One of his older sisters was with them. Her name always escaped him.

His oldest sister, Sonia, was out of the picture too. She had gone her own way again, as she often did. Sonia was an intelligent, feisty twelve-year-old who had learnt to look after herself. She popped back every so often to check on her mother and to try to persuade her to leave her father if they were together, and to try to keep her off alcohol if they were not.

The three of them – Wagner, his mother and the sister with no name – gathered up cardboard, folded it flat, piled it up and, when they had enough, tied it into bundles with string. They waited until there was a lull in the traffic and crossed the road, carrying their awkward-shaped bundles to the island in the middle of the highway. They waited for another lull and crossed to the other side. Wagner had safely reached the pavement when his mother turned back. He turned too. His sister had dropped her doll. It lay on the Avenida Brasil and she ran to pick it up. His mother ran after her, her arms outstretched. They both ran into the path of a Volkswagen Variant – Wagner could always remember cars better than names; his mind seemed to shy away from attaching names to the people he had lost, or who had caused him harm.

Wagner fainted, keeled over right there on the pavement. If his father was not in jail, he did not hear about the deaths in time for the funeral. Sonia did not hear about them until much later. Wagner was taken in by a woman in the *favela*, Teresa. 'She beat me, but not much. She wasn't so bad.' One day Sonia and his father turned up to try to retrieve him. Teresa did not want to let Wagner go – perhaps she was fond of him, perhaps he was simply useful to her – and she threatened his father with a knife. Wagner's father was a big man and more than a match for Teresa, but he felt that he had done his duty by asking for his son back, after all, child-rearing was not men's work, and he went away again when she refused. Teresa died of cancer soon after and Wagner was passed on to another woman, Estelita. When she was drunk, Estelita would beat him unrestrainedly. Wagner still had a dent in his skull and a thin scar on his stomach, which he said were wounds inflicted by her. She kept him naked and locked him up in the yard to prevent him from running away. One day she beat him so badly that the neighbours called the police. Wagner remembered being pulled out of the yard from under the gate.

The authorities transferred him into FUNABEM – the Rio orphanage system. There he was kept in hospital for several months because he was so malnourished, and he had broken bones that needed to heal. Without papers or anyone to confirm his surname, they gave him the common Brazilian name 'dos Santos' and, estimating his age to be seven, suggested a birthday, 5 June 1971. The social worker's report for the year of his entry into the orphanage noted that Wagner was a 'very depressed child, and blocked with regard to information about his family.'

★

'Go on,' said Wagner. 'Read it. What does it say?'

Wagner's FUNABEM papers had been missing for many years. There had been no record of him ever being in the system. The orphanages had been closed down shortly after he left and piles of papers had been left to lie around on the floors of abandoned buildings. Now that his papers had turned up again, he was curious.

'The case of a pupil aged twenty-one, from an illegally constituted and split family: father was serving a sentence for setting fire to a house and mother was killed, together with one of her daughters, on the Avenida Brasil when they went out to sell cardboard...

'...Your father set fire to a house?'

'Could have done,' said Wagner. He searched for a memory. A cloud shifted. 'Ah! Yes!' he said. He sounded really pleased. 'Yes! My father set fire to my mother's house!'

'And you remember that?'

'Yes! We were in it!' he said excitedly. 'I've still got the scar on my hand. Look!' He held out his enormous hand. There, covering a third of his palm, was the thick rippled scarring of a burn mark.

★

The orphanage that Wagner was transferred to when he was about fifteen was a three-hour drive into the interior of the state near a small town called Morro Azul. By now it had been six or seven years since he had last had any contact with his family. His older sister, Sonia, had visited him two or three times in his first couple of years in the institution, but the last time he had seen her she had been heavily pregnant, and then she had stopped coming. It was from Sonia that he knew his real name, Wagner Dias de Araújo, but he was used to dos Santos, and preferred to keep it. There was some story about a younger sister who had been given up for adoption, but if he had ever known her name, or understood where and how she fitted in, he did not know any more. Sonia had given him a photo, but he had lost it.

The loss of his family was a constant ache in his life. 'I spent my life without a father or a mother. I really missed that.' Children were often put into FUNABEM because their families could not support them. Some still had both parents and many were in contact with siblings or aunts or grandparents. They had visitors and sometimes went home for weekends or holidays. Wagner was unusual in being so alone. If he ever had a home, it was FUNABEM.

The last step in the chain of FUNABEM orphanages was the Instituto Rodolfo Fuchs. Rodolfo Fuchs had been a German pastor who believed that poor and abandoned boys could be saved by a combination of God, nature and work. He bought some land in the soft velvety hills of Rio de Janeiro state and built a pleasingly symmetrical, colonial-style building with large airy dormitories which were laid with Portuguese floor tiles, and established an orphanage which was also a working farm. When he died his niece donated the property to FUNABEM and he was remembered in the forecourt by a bronze bust.

It was beautiful countryside. Rivers wound their way between the hills and banana groves fanned out in the valleys. Men with infinitely-lined faces drove carts drawn by scrawny mules through sleepy little towns. Wagner did not come across as a country boy, but he had spent his adolescence surrounded by green hills and farm animals and he had been happy there. The boys worked in the mornings, and received a small salary. All the work on the farm was done by the boys, including the cooking and the cleaning. Wagner worked in the bakery. There were workshops where boys learnt other skills such as carpentry and metalwork. 'Everything I know, I learnt there,' said Wagner. He was the goalie on the football team and played percussion in the samba band. There was a swimming pool and a hall where they had dances to which they invited girls from the girls' orphanage.

He made it sound like an unflawed idyll, but every so often something dark would drop into the conversation. He once mentioned in passing that he had often been beaten in his first orphanage because he regularly wet his bed until he was ten. Such rare references fell lightly, because violence had been such a constant in Wagner's life that he was ambivalent about certain manifestations of it. It was all a matter of degree. He thought of rape as something that happened in the natural order of things. He said that it was fairly common for the older boys to rape younger boys when they came in from another orphanage: 'It was just like in the army.' He said that he himself had never been raped: 'At my first orphanage there wasn't any of that. It was later that it was bad. By that time I'd grown big. I knew how to defend myself.' Rape was something that happened to the weak and friendless, and Wagner was never friendless. It was the gift granted him instead of family – he could make friends with just about anyone.

'I always tried to be the kind of person who looked out for the weaker kids,' he said. Then, with a shrug of his shoulders, 'But at that time I had no idea about psychology. To me it was simply survival of the fittest.'

Apart from such occasional asides, Wagner spoke glowingly about the place. It was where he learnt right from wrong. He was respected there; he was made a prefect, and often referred to that responsibility with pride. Ultimately, it was what separated him from the Candelária kids. 'I really respected my teachers. I had discipline. I had rules. If I hadn't, I would have been like the Candelária kids. I understand that where I place my foot the other has to follow. They didn't. They were free.'

With hindsight, Wagner saw FUNABEM as a saving grace. His memory emphasised the qualities of 'structure' and 'dignity' and 'respect'. But Wagner was far too much of a party lover to have been half as serious as he liked to portray himself when recalling the orphanage. There was a window in the dormitory out of which he and his friends could drop onto a low roof and into the yard and from there walk the ten kilometres to Morro Azul. On a Saturday night there was often a *forró* where couples turned and turned under a corrugated iron roof to the teetering accordion-based rhythms of the North-East. Afterwards the boys would walk back again, to be found in bed when the doors opened for their wake-up call.

Wagner's childhood friend, Guilherme, had a less rose-tinted view of FUNABEM. 'Have you ever been in a prison?' he asked. 'Well, that's what it was like, only a little less heavy.' He had first met Wagner when they were about twelve, in an orphanage in Caxias. They met on the football pitch, where they were friendly rivals. At other times they held their distance: 'When you live in an orphanage you have to keep your friendships separate. You can't be friends with just anyone. It's a law of survival. You look after what's yours and live your life.'

It was when they were transferred to Rodolfo Fuchs that they became close friends. In Caxias it had been 'survival of the fittest', but in Rodolfo Fuchs, 'it was dog eat dog! Captive dogs!' Wagner and Guilherme found themselves sticking together. Like Wagner, Guilherme had only praise for the staff, 'They taught us as if we were their own children.' But there were four hundred boys aged between fifteen and twenty, a hundred to each dormitory. They formed their little groups and watched each others' backs. 'You depended on each other, always helped each other out. If one had a fight, the other took the blows with him. You always slept close to each other. If you got something for yourself you got it for the other. Wagner and I didn't get into fights easily. What we liked was football and samba. Wagner was always a joker. He always talked a lot and clowned around.'

Guilherme left Rodolfo Fuchs before Wagner did. He had family to go to and he had already met his future wife. He had been called up for National Service, which was, he said, 'Exactly like school only with a uniform.' He and Wagner lost touch. The next time Guilherme saw Wagner was on the evening news. 'I was shocked,' he said. 'I was shocked and I was scared. Because what happened to him involved the police, and here in Rio the police... You know how it is. So I was scared, because I thought that because we were connected it might affect me. Investigations and all...' Guilherme had had many years of keeping his head down. He waited for the dust to settle.

Guilherme was a stocky black man. At Rodolfo Fuchs he had worked with the cattle. He had a deep comfortable voice, and it was easy to picture him talking soothingly to the slow animals. He had been born on a hillside *favela* and had always kept in touch with his family. Now he lived with his wife and children in a secure and scrupulously clean apartment in town. Over the dining table, above a vase of silk lilies, was a poster with the words of the 23rd Psalm:

> *The Lord is my shepherd; I shall not want.*
> *He maketh me to lie down in green pastures:*
> *He leadeth me beside the still waters.*
> *He restoreth my soul:*
> *He leadeth me in the paths of righteousness for his name's sake.*

Yea, though I walk through the valley of the shadow
of death, I will fear no evil: for thou art with me;
Thy rod and thy staff, they comfort me.
Thou preparest a table before me in the presence of
mine enemies;
Thou anointest my head with oil; my cup runneth over.

Surely goodness and mercy shall follow me all the days of
my life: and I will dwell in the house of the Lord for ever.

'Unfortunately Wagner didn't have family,' said Guilherme. 'If he'd had family he wouldn't have been in this situation.'

When Wagner remembered the Candelária kids he saw the fate that he had escaped. But when he looked at Guilherme, he saw the fate that had been stolen from him. It was what he had imagined for himself, what he still dreamt of: a wife, children, steady job, home. It had been within his grasp. He had always been lucky, he said. He had always 'given off a good vibe'.

Guilherme pointed to the window. 'It's raining today,' he said, 'but this city can be wonderful. If you see it from above, the city is beautiful. But the beauty is all on the surface. From below it's all rotten.'

3

Real Life

THERE WAS FUNABEM and then there was the world outside. Because Wagner had no family, he rarely went out of the orphanage and was kept there for longer than most boys. He was nineteen by the time he left, but not a very mature nineteen. 'I had no knowledge of the world outside. I had some idea because I went out sometimes, but I knew nothing about the day-to-day business of finding work, paying rent, buying clothes – the school dealt with all that.' At nineteen, he was still only halfway through the Brazilian first grade.* He had always been a joker in class – the kind of kid, as Guilherme remembered, who liked to distract the others. His discharge papers commented, almost with a note of regret, that 'his disciplinary conduct was merely satisfactory'. But, in a country where, in the year of his discharge, a fifth of the adult population was illiterate, it was not as poor of an achievement as it might sound. He could read and write, and was always grateful for his education.

Before he left, the orphanage set him up with a job at a nearby hotel – 'legal employment' said his discharge papers, which meant proper documentation: employment card, health care and

---

* The eight stages of the first grade are aimed at children from seven to fourteen.

pension contributions. The Hotel Fazenda Caluje nestled among the hills surrounded by trees. It offered middle-class *Cariocas* – residents of Rio – a taste of Brazilian ranch life. Guests could ride horses, milk cows and drink locally distilled *cachaça* at the poolside bar. Wagner did a little bit of everything: kitchen work, cleaning and landscaping. As always, he quickly made friends and his employers were happy with him. They found him to be a hard worker. But it was all a little too quiet for Wagner. There was no one to play samba with, and, after eleven years spent with the constant movement and noise of hundreds of boys, the quiet mornings were strange and unnatural to him. He also found that after the deduction of board and lodging from his pay packet there was very little left. He felt that there must be more to life than this. Wagner was in touch with some of his old FUNABEM friends and they seemed to be having a lot more fun than he was. After about a year at the hotel the pull proved too strong. He packed in his job and left for the capital.

He landed in Vila do João, a government re-housing initiative gone wrong, just off the Avenida Brasil. The houses had been built in a grid on perfectly flat ground and painted brightly in different colours. A tree had been planted in front of every house so that in time its branches would spread over each front yard and give shade from the baking sun. By the time Wagner moved in the state had moved out, and the houses had begun the process of improvisation and upwards expansion that gives Rio's shanty towns their Legoland appearance. The streets had begun to break up, the rubbish accumulating in the ditches. The residents stole their electricity and bought their gas from the *tráfico* – the drug gangs – who brought it into the *favela* with a kickback to the police. The trees had been ripped out by the *meninos*. This innocuous, almost affectionate term, *meninos* – 'boys' – was how the residents referred to the drug traffickers who controlled their community. Why they had ripped out the trees, no one could say. It was the sort of thing they did. A couple of trees had survived where the main streets crossed and had grown large and round and broad with fleshy, oval leaves. Each provided shade to a tiny concrete-bounded seating area with room for four inbuilt tables. Here people leaned or sat on the circular wall and watched groups of men play cards and chess, while music blasted from the loudspeakers in the open boot of a car.

'When there's no shooting the *favela* is like Maracanã Stadium,' said Wagner. He was sharing two rooms with sixteen other boys, mainly ex-FUNABEM pupils. *Favela* life energised him. In every bar and every corrugated iron-roofed stall was a large loudspeaker playing *forró* or samba or rap; layers of competing music drowned out the traffic noise from the Avenida Brasil. The *favela* fizzed with story and intrigue, a heady mix of drug faction politics, police corruption, day-to-day survival and good, old-fashioned bed-hopping. The air was as thick with gossip as it was with heat and dust: who was in, who was out, who was going to get himself killed the way he was going, and who had just been found by the roadside twisted in rigor mortis with a bullet in his head.

The *favela* was a complex dynamic. Most *favelas,* or 'communities', as the residents preferred to call them, were technically illegal. So, although about a third of the population of Rio de Janeiro lived in them, supplying the city with factory and construction workers, cleaners and maids, the state was absent. They were not on the grid for gas, electricity or water; the post was not delivered there. Often they were not on the city bus routes, and residents relied on fleets of white Volkswagen Kombi vans to travel from place to place. This vacuum was occupied by the *tráfico*, and most Rio *favelas* were controlled by one of three warring drug factions.

Favela residents had an ambivalent relationship with the traffickers. On the one hand, most tried to stay out of it and get on with the business of working and feeding their families, but they were intricately interconnected with the *tráfico* whether they wanted to be or not. For a start, everyone knew everyone, so the *meninos* were just that – little boys that the community had watched grow up. You might be friends with their grandmothers; you might even be one of their grandmothers, aunts, uncles, stepfathers or cousins. Then, the *tráfico* was the only administration you had. If you fell foul of the *meninos* they might cut off your gas, kick you out of the community or kill you. They would arbitrate disputes, hand out cash to the needy. The whole community was interwoven with the *tráfico* in a web of need, fear, kinship ties and grace and favour.

Most *favelados*, while disapproving of the *tráfico*, held the police to be the greater criminals. The police took kickbacks on everything that came in and out of the community, including cocaine. They also controlled the flow of arms. The inhabitants of the *favelas* had learnt to live with gun battles between police and traffickers. Often people, 'innocents', were caught in the crossfire and were wounded or killed. Sometimes the police would invade one community, shoot a few people, confiscate arms and drugs, then sell them to a rival community with whom they had cut a better deal.

The greatest criminals of all, though, were perceived to be the politicians. The traffickers were rich by the standards of the *favela* but that translated into little more than fancy sneakers, and they were usually dead by the time they were twenty-five. Meanwhile the police were living out in the suburbs in modest homes and driving second-hand cars. The drug war was fought in the *favelas*, but it was not in the *favelas* that anyone was making money out of the tonnes of cocaine flowing down from Colombia into Brazil.

The *meninos* might be criminals, but they were *their* criminals. As Wagner put it: 'When you see a poor drug trafficker stealing, you don't see it in the same way as when you see a politician stealing, who doesn't need to steal.' And so, two million *Cariocas* lived with a double standard and had their day-to-day lives regulated by a small group of cocaine-dealing, gun-wielding, testosterone-charged adolescents.

'It's difficult living in the *favela* when there are tensions,' Wagner explained. 'But when there are no problems it's excellent. It's a party, a festival, a football game; it's everything. The drug traffickers themselves don't organise much. The residents and the residents' association organise a lot of things and the traffickers give them the money.

'No one forces you to go into the *tráfico* – you do it if you want to. I've had trafficker friends, but I've never held a gun, because that's how it starts. Your friend will say, "Hold my gun for a moment, I've just got to do something." It becomes a habit. He has confidence in you because you give the gun back. After a while he'll start shooting. "You have a go." You start shooting. Before you know it you've got a gun at your neck.' The traffickers had the status, the women and the money, but already Wagner had the suspicion of politics that would later underpin his view of the world: 'What the trafficker is concerned with is power. He's like a politician. And just like a politician he doesn't change anything much.' Wagner saw the power struggles and betrayals and early deaths. It was not for him.

Like anyone with dark skin who lived in the *favela*, however, keeping clean was not enough to protect you from prejudice or from police incursions. The place that Wagner and the other boys were renting had not so long ago been the building from which drug traffickers had conducted their business. The traffickers had moved to another location, but the police did not like large groups of young men in one place, and every so often they broke in late at night and beat them up a little, just to keep them on their toes. Wagner always said that the night raids were motivated by pure evil. He believed that evil was an energy that took hold of people. There was no point in trying to over-analyse motives. He depicted the raids as a sort of cathartic exercise, in which drunken police could vent their anger against the *favela* by picking on a non-threatening target. There must have been some petty criminality and drug use in such a large group of boys, but they were small fry, and the police were known to use bullying tactics to soften up potential informants, so maybe there was more to it than Wagner cared to dwell on.

Whatever the reason, Wagner did not let it bother him too much at first. He was far too busy. He had work covering shifts in a bakery, and on many nights he climbed onto a rickety bus and rattled his way into the city to work a fifteen-hour shift which started at midnight. When he was not working in the bakery in the formal economy, he worked in the informal economy as a street vendor. He bought himself a suitcase which folded out into a table. 'It's easy to work as a street vendor in Brazil. If you buy in bulk it works out cheap. If you buy fifty bottles of water, you only pay for thirty. If you buy six units of sweets you only pay for four. So I did that. I took the money I had, invested it, and set up at the Novo Rio bus station. I arrived at seven in the morning and left at ten. If the police came, I shut my suitcase and off I went.'

His suitcase broke, but a colleague at the bakery put him onto a job as a security guard. Wagner fit the bill perfectly: 'I was tall, broad and good-looking.' He was exactly what the upper classes wanted sitting in the guard box next to their high gates in lovely beachside Barra da Tijuca. Famous people came and went. He had a blue uniform and a torch, and a bike with which to patrol the perimeter of the complex of beachfront apartments. At night he pedalled through the gardens. Purple orchids dripped from the trunks of fan-leafed trees. The sea sang.

★

Eunice remembered Wagner well. She had lived in Vila do João for twenty-five years. It was a great place to live. 'Look how quiet it is!' By 'quiet' she did not mean quiet. A number of musical genres were competing with each other at full volume. She meant no gunfire, no police raids, no drug faction wars, no thirteen-year-old boys sitting on street corners caressing machine guns. And it was even on the bus route into town.

Still, the *favela* was not what it used to be. You could not just come and go as Wagner once had. Entering a *favela* as a stranger involved a mysterious invisible process whereby your host informed the residents' association, who in turn cleared it with the *tráfico*. When Wagner had lived here, it had been possible to visit *favelas* controlled by rival drug factions. Not any more. The city had grown more and more factionalised and violent, the police incursions more and more vengeful. Its inhabitants, world famous for their mellow approach to life, had become more hysterical. The beautiful lilt of Brazilian Portuguese had become shrill with incredulity.

'Wagner was always on his way somewhere,' remembered Eunice, as she stood outside the house where Wagner had once lived with the boys. 'The police bothered them a lot,' she said. The house was now three storeys high. Eunice stepped back into the street and clapped her hands. A face looked out from an upper floor, pale and frightened. It disappeared again.

In a neighbouring house a couple of women leant in their doorway, people-watching, absorbing the heat. Eunice called out, 'What's the name of the girl who lives in there?'

One of the girls made a slight movement, a sort of unpeeling from the doorjamb. 'Salete.'

'Ô!' yelled Eunice to the upstairs window. 'Salete! *Sa-le-chee!*'

Eunice adjusted her glasses. One of the arms had broken off. She could not see without her glasses and was saving up for a new pair – she thought it would take her another three months.

Eventually a terrified woman came down to the metal gate, opened it a fraction and clung to it, looking up and down the street. She was Jorginho's sister. Jorginho had lived there with Wagner, or had rented it to Wagner – or something. Salete could not remember Wagner. She could not remember anything. It did not seem safe to her to do so.

'Where did they find your brother's body?' asked Eunice, conversationally, to break the ice.

'Up by the university.'

'Ah!' Eunice sympathised. 'The university. Did you get to bury him?'

'We did.'

'Ah! You were lucky. Haven't you got any photos?'

'No. The *meninos* took everything.'

'And Berg. He lived here too, didn't he?'

Salete admitted to remembering Berg. Perhaps because Berg was dead too. And there was another boy, Mané – he had moved to Vila do Pinheiro. He might know more. Eunice thanked her and moved on.

Salete had made Vila do Pinheiro sound as if it were another world. And, technically, it was. Three blocks down was the road that exactly demarcated the border between Vila do João and Vila do Pinheiro. Vila do Pinheiro was dangerous. '*Lá, o bicho pega mesmo!*' – 'The beast really attacks there!' – said Eunice, using the national euphemism for drug faction or death squad torture and murder. However, it was controlled by the same faction as Vila do João, so Eunice was free to go there. She went from door to door in a row of dilapidated apartment blocks. 'Do you know a Mané, supposed to live in this block?' It was Sunday. The smell of caramelised garlic and barbecued beef filled the air. Some children skipped in the street, puffs of white dust at each jump. Eventually, a girl carrying a canary in a cage confirmed that Eunice was standing outside Mané's door. No one was in. She shoved a note under the door, leaving a phone number.

Why had she asked Salete about burying Jorginho?

'They don't leave bodies nowadays.' She said, matter-of-factly. 'They microwave them.'

'What?!'

'They chop them up and put them in a pit and pour petrol all over them and set them alight. They don't leave *anything*!'

'What did he do?'

24

'Oh ... *something*. He must have been an *X-9* – a police informant – or something.

'And Berg?'

'AIDS.'

Eunice lived with lots of cats. There was a huge hole where she was renovating her front room. For now her home was an unpainted grey-rendered room with an enormous bed. An extension lead ran to a bare light bulb in the centre of the ceiling and the remaining space was taken up by a sewing machine and a set of bookshelves full of textbooks: English and French language courses, legal texts. She was taking an evening course in civil law.

She had not been able to believe it when she saw Wagner on the television. 'No one who knew him would have expected it. He was working and everything!'

The following day Mané phoned. He sounded frightened. Whoever had given his name must have been mistaken. He could not remember anything about anyone.

4

Come-Gato/Ruço

In FUNABEM, WAGNER had known a boy called Come-Gato – Cat-Eater. There were several versions as to how he acquired this name. In one he was abandoned as a small child and killed a cat for food in order to survive. In another, his grandmother regularly served cat for dinner and he ate it with relish.

When he came into the orphanage he was small and skinny. 'He really suffered,' remembered Wagner. 'A lot of people used to beat him up because of that story about him eating cats. You know what children are like. He was very withdrawn.' Dodging the beatings made him agile and a very fast runner. 'Come-Gato wasn't homosexual when I first knew him,' Wagner commented, casually. 'He turned homosexual later, because he was raped at school.'

One day, in the late 1980s, like many of Wagner's fellow FUNABEM pupils, Come-Gato ran away. It would be a couple of years before Wagner saw him again.

Come-Gato headed for the city, and, like most of the flotsam that drifted into the state capital, he washed up at Candelária Church. This vestige of colonial splendour now formed a traffic island, overshadowed by the concrete flyover of the perimeter highway that brought traffic into the city, and by the shiny high-rises of the financial district. It was almost as old as the city itself. The story went that, at the beginning of the seventeenth century, a Spanish ship, the *Candelária*, ran into a storm. The men on board swore an oath that, if their lives were spared, they would build a chapel dedicated to Our Lady of the Candelária. Their prayers were heard. They sailed gently into a bay of white sands and lush green hills and built their offering of thanks.

It had evolved into a grand, white-domed church with massive doors on which were sculpted plump Caucasian cherubs floating on clouds. They looked down beatifically upon the scrawny black kids who scampered about on the flight of steps below them. On the forecourt of the church was a fountain in which an incongruous female nude knelt in supplication. It was there that the homeless bathed and washed their clothes. Candelária was a triage point. It was where the homeless found their bearings before moving on to other locations in the city, but there was also a permanent group of street kids living there, and Come-Gato stayed put. They lived where the broad Avenida Presidente Vargas ran out of land and veered suddenly around Candelária Church and under the flyover. They sheltered where the flyover met briefly with the ground, providing them with a cave at the edge of the road. It was too low to stand, and so they squatted there, oblivious to the din of traffic overhead, and to the buses rattling so fast around the bend that they displaced blasts of air which shook the cardboard walls of their homes. They lived with the stench of petrol fumes and human excrement, which they obliterated in the hazy highs of glue-sniffing.

The number of children and adolescents in the group fluctuated, rarely rising above twelve. Their individual histories

27

were varied combinations of four themes: they had been abandoned by impoverished parents; they had fled physical or sexual
abuse; they had absconded from FUNABEM or the juvenile
detention system; or they had simply been born on the streets
and there they had stayed. The misery of their short lives made
them all but invisible to the swarms of middle classes which
milled around the city centre during the day. The kids came into
focus only when they stole, which they did frequently. And so
they darted in and out on the edge of the city's consciousness,
dashing in to beg for food or to grab a handbag. They were
always, at the very least, an annoyance. Sometimes they could
be dangerous and frightening.

Come-Gato had grown up in the group. In 1992 he was
nineteen. He was still small and skinny, but wiry and streetwise,
all tight skin over adolescent muscle, with sharp, knowing
European features under a tangle of bleached hair. It was the
peroxide that had given him a new nickname, 'Ruço', which
described the shade of smoker's orangey-blond that came from
bleaching hair that was not meant to be blond. Come-Gato's
sidekick, Turinha, was another permanent fixture in the group.
They decided who was in, who was out. They made the rules.
Both dressed like girls in tight shorts and little halternecks which
exposed their bellies. Turinha was a voluptuous black boy, who
made a lot of his full mouth. Together they lived out a fantasy
of domesticity with their following of children. Under the
viaduct they mapped out kitchens and living rooms in cardboard
and played at mummies and daddies. Come-Gato and Turinha
were the 'mothers'. They chose their 'children' from the younger
members of the group, the seven-, eight- and nine-year-olds.
Older boys were taken on as 'husbands'. In his role as wife and

mother, Come-Gato/Ruço took on yet another name: Priscilla.
They were sexually promiscuous: 'husbands' were kicked out
of the group and replaced, and they had sex with their 'children'.

Their lives were influenced by the energies of the *Orixás* –
the African spirits who were bound with forces of nature and
had been grafted by slaves on to Catholic Saints. They formed
part of the belief system of millions of Brazilians. It was a direct
relationship, and the children chatted about their *Orixás* as
though they saw and heard them: Oxalá the omnipresent, Ogum
of roads and grasslands, Oxóssi of the forests, Xangô of the
stones, Oxum of the waterfalls, Iansã of winds and storms,
Iemanjá of the sea, Obaluaiê of the earth, Nanã of still water
and rainwater.

The world of the Candelária kids bumped against others.
Sometimes people sought a way in. One such person was Marjorie
Botelho. She was studying psychology at Rio University at the
time and had just left home. She used to visit the *Centro Cultural*
which stands opposite Candelária Church. It was a beautiful
public space which took you through a high arch of belle
époque wrought iron gates into a circle of cool marble. There
people sat on curved steps under a high galleried dome.
Exhibitions were held there, delicate drawings graced the walls.
Browsers in the art bookshop lifted books from the shelves and
carefully turned the vibrant pages. Espresso cups clinked gently
on saucers.

Leaving home had not been a happy experience for Marjorie.
Perhaps that was why the Candelária group drew her attention.
She nicknamed the group *'uma boa'* because they would watch
the women walking past and call out *'uma boa!'* – 'gorgeous!' They
would snatch handbags as much for the prettiness of the object

29

as for its contents. One day Marjorie cleared out some old clothes and brought them to Turinha and Come-Gato. They started talking. She was deeply affected by their situation, by their abandonment. 'I think it was to do with my idea of the world, with what I thought about what I wanted for the country, for people. They were children!' She started visiting them regularly. She took them to the beach, to the theatre. 'I became a bit obsessed about doing something stable with that group of kids.'

At the time, Marjorie was barely more than a kid herself, light-skinned and freckled with a crop of dyed blonde hair. She kept a photo album of her time with the Candelária kids and in image after image she looked out through enormous glasses from the middle of the group. The kids were always posed, grinning, their hips pushed into feminine angles.

One day in 1992 the Candelária group received a threat from a couple of plain-clothed policemen. They told them to clear out of there; there was going to be trouble. They took the threat seriously and moved on. Up in the hills a man called Joãosinho 30, a Carnaval impresario extraordinaire, had set up a project for orphaned and abandoned children. Joãosinho 30 was the power behind one of Rio's most famous samba schools, Beija-Flor. His idea was that Carnaval was the perfect medium to pass on practical skills. It was brilliant: draw the children in with music and dancing and sequins and feathers. The kids loved it. Carnaval was a huge industry. There was work to be done and trades to be learnt at every level from sewing to logistics. He called the project *Flor do Amanhã* – Tomorrow's Flower. It was bursting with optimism.

Marjorie used to drop by at the project to visit Turinha and Come-Gato. There she met a lawyer, Cristina Leonardo. Cristina was a raven-haired, red-lipsticked explosion of energy, who always had ten things on her mind at once. She ran around calling everyone 'Darling!' and 'My Love!' in a resonant gravely voice: '*Oi Querida! Ó Meu Amor!*' She was a political animal, and, as a lawyer, understood the importance of paper. Many of the children who turned up at the project had no papers of any kind. Cristina was concerned with citizenship. Without papers, the children would never be able to break into the bureaucracy within which they would have access to state shelters, health care and employment. They called her the '*Tia dos documentos*'. *Tia* – Auntie, or *Tio* – Uncle, being how all Brazilian children referred to all friendly adults.

Wagner's orphanage visited the project. It had a samba group in which Wagner played percussion. There he bumped into Come-Gato. If Wagner noticed that Come-Gato was now dressed as a girl, he never thought to mention it. But he was struck by his expression: 'His face had hardened,' he said. 'He must have been on the streets for a long time.' Wagner went back to the orphanage. *Flor do Amanhã* folded in a storm of allegations of paedophilia or fraud or both. The kids came down from the hills and back on to the streets. It was like the Pied Piper in reverse.

The Candelária group had other regular visitors. For several years a shift from a team of caseworkers employed by a non-governmental organisation called the *Centro Brasileiro da Defesa dos Direitos da Criança e do Adolescente* – Brazilian Centre for the Defence of the Rights of the Child and Adolescent – had spent a couple of hours with the kids at Candelária every Monday and Wednesday night. The enormously long title of this organisation attached to a modest but efficient project focused on sexual health. Candelária was one of a number of groups of street kids in the centre of the city on which the *Centro Brasileiro* kept an eye. Brazil took the problem of AIDS very seriously. In 1992, projections for the spread of the disease were alarming. Street children were at extremely high risk for contracting and spreading HIV.*

The *Centro Brasileiro* teams were led by a young psychologist, Andrea Chiesorin. She had a passion for people and an extraordinary facility for putting them at their ease. She had invited a number of psychology students to work with the street children. Marcelo Ferreri, one of the caseworkers, found that his contact with the street population transformed his view of his home city. 'My world turned around. I didn't walk through the centre of the city the way I did before. I looked at a square and tried to see where the manhole covers were, because I knew that the children stored their clothes there. I tried to see where there was an outlet of water to see where they bathed. It looked at my surroundings totally differently. And also, it was a time of utopian dreams, of wanting to do something for others, for the children, do something that the state wasn't doing. Confront the state because it took no action.'

Andrea was particularly fascinated by the unusual way in which the Candelária group was structured. One day, bantering with the kids, she came up with term '*gay-rotas*', a pun on the Brazilian word for girl: *garota*. They liked it, and the word stuck. They were atypical not only for their transvestitism and their imitation of the family ideal, but also for how unusually well organised they were. 'It was a group that never went hungry, because they'd made an arrangement with the local restaurants

---

* Brazil's assault on the spread of HIV/AIDS is one of the country's success stories. It is the only developing country to provide universal access to free retroviral drugs.

so that they wouldn't clash with them. At around 3.30, 4.00 o'clock they used to go to get the leftovers from the restaurants. But it was in the most disgusting form possible – they mixed all the food together, put it into large tins and gave it to the kids. So they had that routine. Come-Gato was someone who was learning to become civilised. He used to summon the children to distribute the food. He understood about glue abuse. Come-Gato had become a teacher. He used to take the glue away from them so that they would eat.'

Every so often Andrea would slip into referring to Come-Gato in the feminine, as if he constantly switched gender in her memory. Over the three years that she worked with the Candelária group, Andrea had invested more in Come-Gato than in any other street kid. He was about seventeen when they met. 'It was interesting because he was someone who really paid attention to us when we talked about AIDS and HIV prevention; when we talked about violence; when we talked about drugs. He started to want to teach and he helped us to work with the other children. For example, wherever we worked we had a code of conduct. When we were around the kids weren't allowed to show up with stolen goods or steal in front of us or use drugs; no glue-sniffing, no cocaine, no cannabis, nothing. What was interesting was that he helped us to maintain this code. So if, say, one of them had stolen something and came close, Come-Gato immediately pointed them out and said, "Get out of here. You're dirt in the eyes of these people!" He did everything he could to allow our work to have some effect. Come-Gato was always responsive to teaching, and I think that that was a result of our work. I remember that when we started working on the "geography of the human body" which we started in order to address the prevention of diseases, so that they would have some idea – in truth it was all work aimed at boosting self-esteem. If they carried out a mugging, it was because they had nothing to lose. The first step was that they should learn to like themselves. And that was one of the things that we did: the fact that we were there, that we listened to the story of each of them and worked towards the reconstruction of their selves. And Come-Gato was a result of our work. Amongst all those that I worked with he was perhaps the one who really understood what it was to teach and who could pass it on. He had limitations, of course, because he dropped out of school so early, but he had the possibility of taking on a civilian, urban life, of being able to work, of being able to have a job, of being able to look after himself.'

As far as many Brazilians were concerned, organizations like the *Centro Brasileiro* only legitimated people living in the streets and exacerbated the problem of street crime, but for Andrea, the glimmer of hope for Come-Gato was a vindication of what she termed 'intervention' on the streets.

★

The year 1992 was important for Rio de Janeiro. The city hosted ECO-92, the UN Conference on Environment and Development, a huge international junket with scores of visiting heads of states and dignitaries. It was considered a triumph. The Brazilian writer Zuenir Ventura commented drily in his book *Cidade Partida* – Divided City – that 'with its long tradition of narcissism, always very sensitive to what other people said about it, the *Cidade Maravilhosa* – Marvellous City – experienced its moment of glory. The gringos were dazzled.' The deployment of the army into the centre ensured a huge reduction in crime 'enflaming fantasies about military occupation of the *favelas* to resolve the problems of drugs and violence' and the sun shone solidly for two weeks. 'There was little to prevent Rio from being confused with paradise ... however, after this truce followed the hangover. In the second half of 1992 everything went back to normal, that is to say, routine violence. And 1993 would be worse.'[1]

Perhaps it was in reaction to this moment of artificial peace that the city grew more violent. For two weeks the middle classes of Rio had enjoyed a First World existence without the imposition of their Third World co-inhabitants. The hotel industry felt it most keenly. The gringos had been dazzled, but it did not last. Tourism was adversely affected by the number of street children in the city. It was rumoured that hoteliers paid extermination squads to kill street children and disperse the groups. 'The threat to the Candelária group was constant,' said Marjorie. 'Tourism was losing out. There was a very large number of street kids. Not just in Candelária, but in the *Zona Sul*.* I don't think that there has ever been such a large number of kids in the street as at that time. It's obvious. There were a large number of thefts and robberies...'

At the beginning of 1993 the head of the *Centro Brasileiro*, Ana Filgueiras, became ill. She knew of Cristina Leonardo's work and liked her political energy. She invited Cristina to take over the running of the organisation, and, at the request of the Candelária kids themselves, Cristina invited Marjorie to join the caseworker teams. It was a difficult adjustment for Marjorie. 'I

---

* 'South Zone' – Rio de Janeiro's famous beachfront districts.

had a big crisis when I joined the *Centro Brasileiro* because I was already installed with that group. I already had an informal relationship – I went with them to the swimming pool, the beach, the theatre. I already had a relationship that was not institutional. And the institution raised this with me. At one stage they took me off Candelária because it was a very emotional relationship.'

In February 1993, just before Carnaval, the group received another threat. They told the *Centro Brasileiro* caseworkers that they were worried about the extermination squads – the *extermínio* – and that they wanted to be taken off the streets. Coming off the streets meant either a return to the family or to be taken into a state institution. The *Centro Brasileiro* spent a lot of energy on trying to find alternatives to the street, but often the children's families were so violent or poor that a return was impossible or undesirable, and for a child who had enjoyed the absolute freedom of life on the streets, a state institution with its rules and regulations was unattractive, so the children often ran away. Whatever had happened to make the Candelária group ask for help must have really frightened them.

Andrea and Marjorie put the wheels in motion and arranged for the group to be received by the judge responsible for minors, so that he might authorise state hostel or orphanage places for them. Unfortunately, two of the group had neglected to admit to Andrea and Marjorie, when asked, that they had outstanding detention orders against them. The judge ordered their arrest there and then. The kids, who were all crowded into the court-room, erupted in fury. Mainly they were angry with Andrea and Marjorie, whom they believed to have been complicit in this betrayal. Andrea and Marjorie, shouting above the din of accusations, felt strongly that the judge might have handled the situation more sensitively. They failed to address him as 'Your Excellency'. A court official reprimanded Marjorie for forgetting her manners. 'He's not the king!' Marjorie yelled. The judge slapped a contempt charge on Andrea and Marjorie: 'You're not *educadoras* – teachers,' he admonished them. 'You're *deseducadoras*.'

The two absconders were taken off to a juvenile detention unit. The rest of the kids dispersed. The *Centro Brasileiro* teams looked for them. For weeks they walked around the Candelária group's favourite haunts, through the maze of cobbled streets of the old town where the paint curled off the panelled double doors and the wrought iron balconies rusted quietly. They looked under flyovers which unfurled over the squares and the derelict warehouses of the docks. There was a scruffy strip of concrete quay behind Candelária where a set of steps led into the water, and where the horizon was demarcated by the slender length of the bridge which joined Rio de Janeiro to the green hills of Niteroi. On sunny days all the street kids of the centre declared a truce and ran up and down hurling themselves into the polluted water, but the Candelária kids had stopped swimming there. On Monday and Wednesday nights the teams went and sat on the steps of the church and waited to see if anyone would turn up. No one did. The Candelária group had gone.

5

Taking Over Candelária

THE CANDELÁRIA KIDS had been gone for about three months. And then around March 1993 they started to reappear, one by one, in the city centre. They never said where they had been or what they had been doing, and if they were still angry with Andrea and Marjorie over what had happened at the juvenile court, they never mentioned it. The group reformed. Marcelo Ferreri, who had been working at the *Centro Brasileiro's* other sites, now started to do shifts at Candelária. Like his colleagues, he was fascinated by the unusual nature of the group. 'I had never had contact with a group that was so free, so abandoned, so much to themselves. I thought that their situation was the most vulnerable imaginable.'

The *Centro Brasileiro* caseworkers were not the group's only charitable visitors. Come-Gato and Turinha had started to mention a woman called Yvonne, who came to see them. They were never very forthcoming about the other parts of their lives – only the moment was real to them – so Andrea was curious about *Tia* Yvonne. She came in the mornings to give them breakfast and to teach, Come-Gato told her.

Andrea thought it sounded odd. And it was odd. Yvonne Bezerra de Mello was what the newspapers would later delight in calling a 'member of the elite', 'a socialite'. She never objected to these labels. She had earned them, not had them handed to her on a plate. Her mother, a single parent, had struggled so that Yvonne could study in Paris, where she acquired a doctorate in linguistics and a Swedish diplomatic husband. It was 1980 before she found herself back in Rio, and she was shocked by what she found on the streets of Copacabana: 'I had to learn the new reality of Brazil.'

Yvonne's second husband was the owner of a chain of hotels. She owned a beautiful, cool, airy apartment in the *Zona Sul*, a weekend house in the country, and a studio where every day she scrubbed the floor clean on her hands and knees so that she could think clearly enough to work on her rounded, fluid sculptures. A couple of mornings a week her driver took her to a bakery where she picked up bread and milk, and he waited patiently in the car while she held her 'street school' on the Candelária Church forecourt.

This did not make her popular with her peers, which was partly why she acquiesced to the 'elite' tag. Yvonne reasoned that her engagement with the street kids highlighted the wilful blindness and cruel indifference of the upper classes: 'I moved up in life. Everyone just looks after themselves. Nobody lifts a finger in this country. The elite took offence. I was crazy. They couldn't co-exist with a crazy woman!'

She liked to present herself as someone who stood alone, but she was not a team player. There were all sorts of people who were working on behalf of Rio's street population, but Yvonne was not looking for allies. She had developed her own methods and set up where and how she wanted to. She sat with the kids in the centre of town for all of Rio to see, dressed simply in shorts and a T-shirt with her hair pulled back into a ponytail. She splashed about in the fountain with them. She believed that education was the key to breaking the cycle of domestic violence and sexual abuse that pushed kids on to the streets. She started with physical contact – hugging, holding – and moved on from there. Before the massacre her acquaintances thought of it as an eccentricity. Afterwards she appeared to them as a troublemaker and defender of criminals and they saw it as a betrayal. People spat at her.

'I began to be *cursed*,' she said. 'I have spent years being *cursed* in Rio de Janeiro.' She used the word in English, hissing the 's', the Portuguese word was too soft to convey her contempt.

In the three months before the massacre something strange began to happen at Candelária. 'The Candelária group had stayed small for several years, between eight and fifteen kids,' said Yvonne. 'Before the massacre it started to swell. Children started to appear from everywhere and anywhere until in July, just before the massacre, there were seventy-two children. I couldn't understand why this was happening all of a sudden.'

According to Cristina Leonardo, two separate incidents led to the sudden rise in numbers. The first was a love story. There was a group of street girls which had based itself in Copacabana. It was an attractive location. Tourism offered opportunities in theft and prostitution. Chivvying this group along with relentless energy was a sixteen-year-old known as *Beth Gorda* – Fat Beth. She was a round-faced girl with a halo of black curly hair who talked incessantly, rippling up and down several octaves of scales, as she bustled about swinging her backside. She was known as a thief, drug pedlar, fantasist and liar, and yet she was remembered with enormous affection. One day a cheerful, pretty, but not-too-bright boy called Rogeirinho went to the beach. Beth wanted him the minute she laid eyes on him, and that was that. Rogeirinho's group was based at Praça Mauá. Beth being Beth, she managed to persuade her group of girls to move from Copacabana, where there were lots of tourists, to Praça Mauá, where there were not.

It did not take them long to realise that Praça Mauá was a much rougher location. Rogeirinho's group was more threatening than the Candelária group. Its members occasionally used knives made of shards of glass to mug their victims. And it was naval territory, which meant that the group lived with the permanent threat of retaliation, not only from military police, but also from naval police.

Beth found that she did not like Praça Mauá after all, but she did not want to go all the way back to Copacabana where she would be too far away from Rogeirinho. Besides, by now, as well as being in love, she was pregnant. She moved with her girls to Candelária, and Rogeirinho came to visit. Beth embraced the happy family fairy tale of the Candelária group and she and Rogeirinho 'adopted' some of the kids.

It was an odd and uncomfortable juxtaposition: a group of girls and a group of would-be girls. But something else was going on. 'At this time,' explained Cristina, 'the *tráfico* invaded Rato Molhado, where Come-Gato had contact with some children, and some people were forced out of the *favela* and ended up on Dias da Cruz Street. Then the security guards chucked the children out of there – they were the little ones – and Come-Gato brought them all to Candelária. That's how those seventy children got together, which was madness!'

★

One night in June 1993, Wagner fell asleep in his guard box and was jolted awake by a furious boss threatening to sack him if it happened again. He was not getting much sleep: there were long shifts at the bakery, night shifts as a security guard, and then there was the more important business of being twenty-one, which involved the pursuit of music and girls. Wagner reacted to his boss as he often did when people wound themselves up: he made light of it. Too light of it – he often laughed when he was nervous. He hung on to his job, but in retrospect it was the point at which his life began to unravel at such speed that later he would be unable to say exactly how and in what order. Brazil was at the tail end of a severe recession and unemployment was high. The bakery shifts had dried up, and now the security firm explained to him that they had to make cuts and it was last in, first out.

In Vila do João, the police raids on Wagner's house had intensified. 'We just carried on and then at one point we began to see that things were getting serious.' Around the same time that Wagner lost his jobs the police broke in one night, put a gun to his head and told him that if they did not all get out of there they would be coming back to kill them. They got out of there. Wagner had nothing to pack.

He moved into the city centre, to Praça Mauá, and became one of those people in every Brazilian city who offer to watch your parked car for some small change. He was now homeless and unemployed. When he made enough money he slept in a cheap bunkhouse, but on some nights he was forced to sleep on the streets. 'I thought, how can a human being fall to this level? Being on the streets, owning nothing. It was...'

But he could not say how it was. He could only shake his head. It was mid-June, 1993. He had just celebrated his twenty-second birthday.

Praça Mauá was only a short walk from Candelária and the street kids meandered between the two places. There were many familiar faces among them from Wagner's FUNABEM days. Come-Gato came and went, and Rogeirinho, Beth's boyfriend, was a fixture at Praça Mauá.

One night the naval police decided it was time to clean up Praça Mauá, and they gave the order for the homeless to clear out. Wagner and the other street kids ended up at Candelária. Even now, Wagner was only a visitor to the group. He was a couple of years older than its leaders and he held himself apart from them, while at the same time being drawn to them. He saw them as 'free'. Wagner's whole upbringing had been regulated by institutions, and he was intrigued by their amorality. They were utterly unburdened by any sense of consequence or of the future. They simply lived.

He did not sleep with the group, who all huddled together at night. There was no longer enough room for them all under the viaduct, so they took over the pavement under the loggia of Safra Bank, diagonally opposite the church. When it was not raining, some of the children slept on the steps of the church. Some nights, when he did not have any spare cash for the bunkhouse, Wagner stayed up to watch over them. He felt protective of the little ones. There was only a handful of adolescents in the group – the rest of them were under twelve. One night while he was there, a rival street group from Cinelândia had come armed with knives to attack them. Wagner towered over most people, he could make quite an impression simply by standing up. He saw himself as someone who looked out for weaker people, 'a kind of Che Guevara'.

'A street kid is an adventurer,' said Wagner. 'He's got nothing to lose and nothing to gain. I knew a lot of bad people when I lived in the *favela*, but I never saw bad in the Candelária kids. They were not dangerous. Yes, they stole. They did it in a way that made them seem like spiders. They could climb whatever they wanted. It was impressive, to see a kid who didn't have any military training scale a wall! I never saw any of them use a knife. One of them stayed in place so that the other could climb on him, and they would form a pyramid so that they could get away.'

As ever, Wagner made no value judgements about criminality when the perpetrators were poor; he neither condoned nor condemned. 'A kid this size!' He held his hand at knee height. 'If you let a kid of this size rob you then you're worse than him! One slap and he'll fall over!' He was being disingenuous. He was the first person to acknowledge that a child who goes on to the streets at seven or eight can be very dangerous by the time he is twelve or thirteen. 'It was one just of those things,' he said, 'a survival technique.'

By July the *Centro Brasileiro* caseworkers were beginning to worry. 'I had the impression that all these children wanted to stay on the streets,' said Marcelo. 'It seemed to be cool to be on the streets, and it was *really* cool to be on the streets at Candelária, because that's where the children were free.'

It was unprecedented and unsustainable. 'I knew exactly what was going to happen,' said Yvonne. 'To the extent that one week before it happened I went to the deputy mayor and said, "Look, if you don't take action this is going to end badly."'

At the *Centro Brasileiro* the atmosphere was tense. Cristina was agitated; her sensitive political radar was bleeping loudly. She called Andrea back from Recife, where she had been attending a conference. She darted from one place to another shouting, 'We need to find out who these children are and get them registered!' It all came back to paper – without paperwork they had no identities. Without identities the juvenile court could not, or would not, do anything for them. Cristina went to the juvenile court judge to ask for a court order to remove the kids to a place of safety. The judge wanted photos, individual details. 'Can't you just send a car round to Candelária?' begged Cristina.

Cristina had never met Yvonne, but she called her too. 'I left her a message, asking her to stop taking the kids breakfast, because she was reinforcing a dangerous situation.' But it was too late for that. Yvonne had a better idea. She turned to Brazil's first emergency service: the media.

Yvonne had invited celebrity journalist, Glória Maria, to do a feature on 'solidarity and love' with the street kids for the nation's favourite TV magazine, *Fantástico*. Cristina was furious. The kids had been enjoying themselves far too much already, and now suddenly they were going to be on *Fantástico*. Cristina and Andrea were there for the filming, to check with the kids that they did not mind. But of course they did not mind, they were delighted. It was the first time the two women had met Yvonne. They were curious about her motivation, and slightly suspicious of her, especially Andrea, who distrusted Globo, the vast, conservative media machine that was Brazil's most powerful media conglomerate. She could not see how this would help the children. However, during the course of the evening, something emerged. It turned out that Come-Gato had family. He had never talked about his parents to Andrea before, but suddenly he had a yearning to see them.

Later that week Andrea offered to drive Come-Gato into the state interior to see his parents. He did not know the address, but they went in one of the *Centro Brasileiro's* Volkswagen vans to the outskirts of Maricá, on the other side of Niteroi. 'It was like a village – a very rural location. When we arrived, they didn't want to see him at first. They were very uncivil towards him. I think it was his aunt who answered the door. And I asked him to stand aside, and I talked to her, told her who I was, reassured her that she shouldn't be afraid, we weren't there to cause trouble, because who knows what his story was. I said that he just wanted to see his parents. And then she calmed down, and they ended up meeting. It was a very cold meeting, very unemotional. He had been enthusiastic. All the way there he told stories. I think that what happened was that he knew that the most difficult thing for his parents would be to accept his homosexuality. I had made him dress a little more discreetly, because he only ever dressed as a woman. I said, "Wear something you like, but make it a bit more discreet." But I think that the biggest obstacle there was the issue of his homosexuality. They kept their distance. I can't remember any demonstration of affection. There was a brother who tried to smooth things out. It was very quick; we weren't there more than forty minutes. Come-Gato was very sad. He was happy to see them, but at the same time I think he thought that he would never go back.'

The *Fantástico* programme was never aired. Still, Cristina believed that 'of all the things that were happening there, that caused the most outrage' – it was as if the cameras had given Globo's seal of approval to an intolerable situation. But at the same time it had given her an idea of her own. If the minors' court would not send someone down to identify the children, then she would secure their personal details on film and try to move things along that way. She thought that she had hit on a solution. She knew that they were running out of time.

Candelária had turned into a permanent street party, and what thousands of Rio de Janeiro's washed and starched workers were seeing in the centre of the city every day, scampering around on the church steps, squatting to defecate, jumping in and out of the traffic, persistently begging, snatching handbags and reeling with glue, was an infestation of human vermin.

'I never asked myself why it happened,' said Marcelo. 'The way things were going it seemed imminent to me. The question was "Who ordered it?" But why it happened − I never asked myself that.'

6

Birthday Party

ANDREA'S BIRTHDAY WAS 20 July. That year it fell on a Tuesday and she had a small party at home to celebrate. Cristina came by in a flurry of warm congratulations and full of her idea of filming the kids.

When Andrea arrived at Candelária the next night she found that the kids were not talking to her. She put it down to the distraction of the camera. The kids were all taking it in turns to recite their names and tell their stories. But after a while the frostiness of the children began to upset her. Come-Gato took her aside to cheer her up and explained to her that the kids were angry that she had had a party and had not invited any of them, and that she should not worry about it. They would forget about it soon enough. They left the mass of children to the camera and went to hide in the calm sphere of the Cultural Centre. Come-Gato loved the Cultural Centre. It was a world that Andrea and Marjorie had opened up for him, much to the irritation of the security guards, who would never have allowed the kids in unaccompanied. Even with Andrea and Marjorie they were not permitted to enter barefoot, so they would share around their flip-flops and go in small groups to see the exhibitions. Sometimes the *Centro Brasileiro* rented the little cinema in there and showed the kids films. Come-Gato liked to choose them.

He was a little sad himself – still disappointed and hurt by his parents' reception of him the week before. Andrea and Come-Gato chatted a little, and then made their way back to the church. Suddenly all the kids were beaming. It was a surprise party for Andrea. They had somehow – Andrea did not like to think quite how – managed to buy chocolate cake and were jumping up and down singing happy birthday. Marcelo was there too and was struck by the force of the love that those damaged and abandoned children felt for Andrea. 'Every feeling of respect and admiration that I have for Andrea is distilled in the way that the children wanted to hold that party for her. It's unforgettable.'

The camera rolled. The light was tinged orange by the street lamps. In the background the fountain shot white light in the air and the children splashed about in the sparks. Beth sat on the steps with her 'children'. Andrea sat there too, her face hidden by a curtain of thick dark hair. There were drummers, banging out the beat to *Sarapatel*, and the kids jumped up and down with their arms around each other's necks, pushing their shouting, smiling faces as close to the lens as they could. Others wheeled around each other in *capoeira* jousts, swaying and balancing on their hands and feet. The camera raked across the faces of the beaming children. Come-Gato posed, stripped to his skinny waist, and slowly and pornographically ate a piece of cake. The harshness of his life showed in every plane of his angular face. At the end of the night, Cristina tucked the video under her arm and took it home, satisfied. The next day she planned to fix an appointment with the minors' judge.

Wagner was there too, in the background as usual. 'Behind the group, detached' was how Marcelo always remembered him. A waiter came along with a guitar and played along. Marcelo kicked a football about on the church forecourt with some boys. They launched the ball out onto the street, not caring about the passing cars and buses.

Andrea always remembered the number of children that night because she counted them before cutting the cake. If she forgot anyone then they really would be offended. There were four cakes. She carefully cut them into sixty-four squares.

'What stays with me,' said Marcelo. 'Is that that was my last night, because I left Candelária and the next time I went back the massacre had happened. It was as if a curtain closed on the party and opened again on the dead.'

★

The next day, 22 July, was one of those days that Rio exists for: clear blue skies, all-enveloping sunshine. The kids woke up still exhilarated by the party of the night before. Come-Gato ordered a clean-up and soon they were all running about, tidying away the mess, washing clothes in the fountain and laying them out to dry on the vents in the church forecourt, scrubbing down the steps of the church and the pavement where they slept. When Come-Gato declared the job done they sat on the pavement and drummed and sang some samba.

There is a photo from that morning, of a group of kids sitting and standing under the loggia of Safra Bank. They did not like to be photographed, so Come-Gato, having spotted the photographer, was showing him the finger. He was wrapped in a grey blanket and huddled up against Beth, who was smoking a cigarette. A small boy was cradling his head in her lap. A boy called Pimpolho, wearing a floppy jumper, had his back to the camera. He was, said Wagner, 'the funniest of them all.' For once,

Wagner was not standing aside, but instead sat right in the middle of the group. He too must have seen the photographer, because he was looking straight at the camera. It was a serene face, high-cheekboned, fine-featured. '*Bonitão*' – good-looking was how Wagner described himself before 'it happened'. He was right. He was a very good-looking young man.

Because they were still in such a festive mood, some of the kids decided to make it a beach day. This was a logistical challenge, because it involved taking the bus. There was no way that such a large group of street kids would be allowed to board a bus, so they decided to split up into smaller groups and all meet up at *Praia da Urca*, the beach which looks onto Sugar Loaf Mountain. Wagner volunteered to take one of the groups, but they were too excited and boisterous. They were thrown off the first bus and had to wait for another one. On the second bus Wagner yelled at a passenger to stop shouting at the kids and they were thrown off the bus again. When the boys were thrown off the third bus, Wagner decided that enough was enough and he stayed on. He told them he would see them at the beach.

Wagner loved the beach. He believed that 'water cleans the soul'. He swam a little, sunned a little, smoked a few cigarettes and waited for the others to turn up. After a couple of hours of waiting he began to feel a little bored and lonely. It was late afternoon. He took the bus back to Candelária.

When he arrived back there was pandemonium. A huge demonstration of chanting trade unionists was marching around the church under waves of red and white banners, while on the forecourt a boy called Neilton was getting a beating from a policeman and a mass of kids were dancing around them, yelling and waving their arms in the air.

Neilton was being arrested because a traffic policeman had believed that he was giving glue to the younger children. Supplying glue was not actually a crime but the policeman, a young man called Marcos Vinícius Borges Emmanuel, took the view that, while it might not be a crime under the penal code, any sensible person could see that it was wrong for seventeen-year-olds to encourage nine-year-olds in their addiction to hallucinogenic substances.

Neilton, however, had not been giving the children glue, but taking it away from them. It was time for the children's food, and it was a rule of the Candelária group that they should not sniff glue at mealtimes because it stopped the little ones from eating properly. So, when Neilton was dragged towards the police car, under the traditional rain of slaps and punches, the Candelária kids had perceived an injustice. They went berserk. Most of them were scrawny, undernourished little things who could be waved off with a feather individually, but there were a lot of them, and their glue buzz made them bold. It was like being attacked by a swarm of imps.

Under siege, the policeman and his colleagues dragged Neilton to the police vehicle. On the way they grabbed one of the more aggressive children and shoved him onto the back seat too. As they began to reverse off the church forecourt, a stone hit the windscreen of the car. It was such a small thing to the thrower, a boy nicknamed Negueba, and it was soon forgotten by the kids. But that small moment of impact, that brief surge of alarm as the glass shattered, had set a huge wave in motion.

Wagner thought it prudent to stay back. He leant against a wall near the Cultural Centre waiting for things to calm down. He watched Neilton and the other kid being dragged to the police car. He saw the car back off the forecourt. He saw Negueba throw the stone. Eventually he wandered over and heard the story about the misunderstanding over the glue.

An hour or two later, Neilton hobbled back from the police station. It was not the Military Police who brought charges, but the Civil Police – the plain-clothes investigative police – who operated out of police stations and were not involved in policing the streets. It was up to the *Delegado* – the police station head – to press charges, but in this case the *Delegado* could not find anything to charge Neilton with, and had waved arresting officer Emmanuel away impatiently. As Neilton left the police station another of the traffic policemen warned him: 'Don't sleep at Candelária tonight. Something's going to happen.' Neilton asked him, 'Just me?' and he said, 'All of you.' No one else took the warning seriously, but Neilton did. He had been in the car. He had sensed the full measure of the policemen's fury. He said he was going to spend the night in Cascadura. But he was in no hurry; he hung around to chat with Wagner.

The excitement soon subsided. The final trickle of demonstrators marched past. The traffic police returned to their cars and went back to their stations. The bank workers and shop assistants streamed out of the high-rises and went home. The street vendors packed up their cases and wheeled them away. The daytimers all retreated back to their homes in the hillside slums, or the hot dusty suburbs, or the sea-cooled *Zona Sul*. After dark the docks, the wide avenues and the narrow side streets of old Rio belonged to the navy, the police and the very poor.

The evening settled around Candelária and the traffic slowed, and so, without doing anything at all, several hours passed and it was late. The kids were bedding down for the night. A couple of boys had climbed onto the roof of the newspaper stall. Come-Gato had taken up his customary place on the pavement, leaning against the shuttered bank. Beth and Rogeirinho slept on the other side of the road, on the church steps. The smaller children slept already. What with the party and the clean-up and the police incident, it had been a very long forty-eight hours, and they slept deeply, some of them on their backs with their arms above their heads like babies. The nights were cooler in July. They lay there in a tangle of grey blankets and dark brown limbs.

But Wagner was hungry. A small group attached themselves to him and they rose to go for dinner. Neilton, Paulo, Gamba-zinho, Ratinho and Wagner trotted across the now quiet Avenida Presidente Vargas and slipped down a side street.

★

'Why did no one believe Neilton's warning?'

Wagner dismissed the question. 'Why would anyone believe that someone was going to kill them?'

It was a very unsatisfactory answer. The group had moved twice before because they had received death threats. And Wagner himself was well aware that threats could be genuine. 'Yes,' he said, in a tone that implied *of course*. 'I knew people who had been killed by the police. But for things like robbery, not for just walking down the street!'

It was surprising that Wagner could have reached the age of twenty-two, leading the life he did, and still share in the *Carioca* mass self-delusion that the police only murdered the murderous. 'Until this happened to me I had nothing against the police. I just thought the police were the police.' But that too was a survival technique. All *Cariocas* were moral contortionists. It was easier for the city to explain away the violence as a war between police and criminals than to grapple with what to do about it.

For whatever reason, the Candelária kids did not take the threat seriously. Perhaps they thought it only concerned Neilton. Perhaps they believed there was safety in numbers. Perhaps they thought that no one would touch them because they were going to be on the television. So they stayed, and they went to sleep.

★

Wagner smoked his last cigarette. He had picked up smoking in the orphanage at the age of ten. He feared addiction of any kind, but could not kick the habit, and was already thinking about where to buy the next pack. A pile of shredded kale lay untouched on his plate. The others – Paulo, Gambazinho, Neilton and Ratinho – were still scraping up their rice and black beans. The bar hummed with strip lighting, music and the murmur of men with bottles of beer in their hands, their feet flat on the floor in thin flip-flops. Wagner filled out his chair. When he pushed it back slightly from the table the plastic creaked.

It would soon be midnight. Neilton repeated that he was not hanging around to see if the police were coming back. The boys stood up to leave. Neilton said goodbye and headed off to Cascadura. Ratinho said he needed to take a shit. Wagner, Paulo and Gambazinho headed off in the direction of Praça Mauá to buy cigarettes, through the warren of dark alleys, picking their way through the rubbish that gathered in the holes in the cobbles. Paulo and Gambazinho still had the loose-limbed dancing walk of boys. Wagner, older and a good head higher than Paulo and Gambazinho, loped alongside them. They emerged in front of the gates of the naval barracks. A young man stood at guard, starched and crisp in his uniform. Wagner paused to tease him about his finery. The guard did not find this funny, which made Wagner laugh. He always laughed when people were taking themselves too seriously. He was still laughing as he turned off Rua Dom Gerardo, a few paces behind the other boys. The street was shuttered up on one side and was poorly lit. There was a car ahead of them. Some men were rummaging around in the boot. It was not clear what they were doing, whether they were taking something out or putting something in. Paulo and Gambazinho had passed the car and Wagner was trying to catch up with them when a voice called out: 'Police!'

The boys turned around. It was obvious, now, that these men were police: the jeans and the shoes; the way they wore their button-down shirts loose over their belts to hide their handguns; the slight swagger that a gun in their belts gave them. One of them had his gun out and was ordering them up against the wall. 'Back! Back! Back!' He pushed at them, lining them up. Wagner's head slammed against the metal shutter and it juddered at the impact. The man was that indeterminate mix of races that Brazilians call *moreno*, and he was shouting, 'Where's Ruço? Where's Ruço?'

Wagner had pulled his employment card out of his pocket and was holding it above his head. 'Look! I've got an employment card! I live in Vila do João. I've got an employment card.' In Brazil the employment card was no mere bureaucratic document. It was how you distinguished yourself from the documentless criminals and proved yourself a worker. You invoked it like an incantation. It was supposed to protect you from vigilante police.

The man snatched the employment card from Wagner's hand, threw it on the ground and stepped on it. It was not a good sign.

'Where's Ruço, you fuckers? Where's Ruço?'

Paulo, the youngest and the most afraid, sobbed, 'He's at Candelária!'

The man walked along the line of boys and hit them all in the face. *Slap! Slap! Slap!* He had to reach up to hit Wagner. Wagner noticed the chip on his front tooth and could smell the alcohol on his breath. He punched him back.

The man swivelled the gun around in his hand and smashed the butt into Wagner's head. Two other men, who had been standing back, watching, almost relaxed, launched themselves at the boys and began to pull them towards the car, screaming obscenities at them.

There was another man – a white man – already in the car. It was small, a beige Chevette, but somehow they pushed all three boys into the back seat, one by one. Paulo and Gambazinho were jammed in behind the driver's seat. Wagner found himself with his face squashed against the window, with a man sitting on top of him, his gun pressed up against Wagner's cheekbone. The man clicked off the safety catch.

A slim black man took the wheel. The car doors slammed shut and the car moved off and out into the wide Avenida Rio Branco. Another car pulled up parallel, and one of the men gestured to it, waving it on, communicating something – a meeting place, perhaps. The other car pulled away. One of the men in the front seat turned to ask, 'Remember me?' But Wagner never knew who he was talking to. Someone laughed and the gun went off.

As Wagner sank out of consciousness he could hear Paulo and Gambazinho screaming. In the front seat one of the men yelled, 'Fuck! Don't shoot in my car!' They started shouting at each other: 'We have to take him to the hospital!'

'No. No. No!'

Through the window, Wagner could see, at the end of the avenue, framed by high buildings, the tall white concrete T of the war memorial on the edge of Glória cove. The war memorial faded, blurring inwards from the edge of his vision. Then all he could hear was a distant ringing, the reverberations of the gun discharging: *ting, ting, ting*. He felt that he was deep under water, that he was drowning. Then there was nothing, nothing at all.

★

Wagner was only able to tell his story in one way. He had told it so many times that he had stripped it of any emotion. He always referred to his shooting elliptically with the word *'aconteceu'* – 'it happened'. At only one point in the story – always in recounting the same detail – his voice would break and he would have to stop himself from crying. The only other clue to the distress that these memories evoked in him was that remembering altered him. The cheeky, irreverent Wagner disappeared and a serious person took his place. Once he said, 'I don't like to live with this person.' And another time that he believed that the act of recollection was wearing out his memory.

The way he told his story was very like the way that civil police condensed information into a witness statement. On their prehistoric manual typewriters, they typed: 'The witness stated THAT he was walking down Rua Dom Gerardo, THAT he was stopped by men claiming to be police, THAT he pulled out his employment card, THAT the man threw it to the ground, THAT the man hit him, THAT...'

Wagner made no concession to anyone who did not have Portuguese as their first language, or an understanding of *Carioca* slang, or a thorough acquaintance with the geography of Rio de Janeiro. So it took a couple of tellings before one very short sentence suddenly leapt out as being significant. It was just two words: '*Eu devolvi.*'

'Wait a minute. Are you saying that you hit him back?'

'Yes.'

'You don't think that it was, um, a bit...'

'Risky?' offered Wagner, helpfully.

'Risky!'

Wagner pulled himself up straight and pushed his weight back in his chair, indignantly. 'Ah! He hits me and I can't hit him back?'

A slap across the face was, apparently, the worst insult a man can pay another. Punching him in the face, kicking him in the stomach, shooting him – these were not insults, but part of the normal business of disciplining, fighting, drug trafficking or policing. But allowing someone to slap your face was equivalent to submitting to sodomy.

'Still, the guy *did* have a gun. It was a reflex action, perhaps?'

'How can I explain this to you? It was him who hit me. I wasn't doing anything. And I hit him back because if you hit someone you get hit back.'

'Perhaps you had not realised how dangerous they were?'

Wagner waved his cigarette dismissively. 'You're in danger every day. Now, the fact that he hit me without me having done anything – that I could not accept. I did nothing for him to hit me in the face! My mother never hit me. When he slapped my face I hit him back.' Wagner jabbed his left cheek with his forefinger. It made a soft indentation. 'Here! Where my mother kissed me!'

It was not clear whether he was talking about his own mother or the ideal of motherhood.

'At the time, did you think they were going to kill you?'

'No.'

But Wagner wanted no misunderstanding about this. 'Whether or not I hit him back, it made no difference to what happened. They were going to kill us anyway. They had to. We would have been witnesses.'

And this brought him back to the point of the story at which his voice always broke and he had to put his hand over eyes: the point at which he woke up and found Paulo and Gambazinho lying dead beside him.

★

With hindsight it had been quieter than usual at Candelária. The newspaper stand had closed up early. There were fewer taxis than was customary. The normally conspicuous security guards had retreated into the shadows.

Come-Gato and Turinha were still awake when the two cars pulled up alongside the pavement where the children slept. Some men got out. One of them went up to one of the concrete pillars of the loggia, unzipped his trousers and urinated against it, a stream of urine so long lasting that later the children recalled it with awe. Then one of the men walked over to Come-Gato.

'Are you Ruço?'

Ruço/Come-Gato gave the man one of his sly, insolent looks and, invoking his real name for the first time in years, said, 'Who's Ruço? My name is Marco Antônio.'

But the man was not looking for an answer. It was a rhetorical question. He knew who Ruço was. He lifted his gun and shot him in the eye. Turinha was already running. The kids woke up and started to run in all directions, screaming. From their position at the top of the steps on the other side of the road, Beth and Rogeirinho could see everything. Having shot their main target, the men started to fire randomly. One boy fell dead near the newspaper stand. The two boys sleeping on the roof of the stand were startled awake and made to jump from the roof. It seemed as if they were shot in mid-air, descending in slow motion to land on the cobbles, already dead. Pimpolho, Beth's favourite, 'the son I loved most',[2] began to run towards her and fell, mid-stride. The man who shot him pointed his gun at her for an instant frozen in time, but he was not there to shoot pregnant girls. Another boy was killed on the church forecourt, falling spreadeagled onto his back.

The men returned to their cars and drove off. Come-Gato lay slumped against the shutters — somehow he was still breathing. Five other boys were dead. The children grouped around them, keening and crying, wanting to make them comfortable. If any of the office cleaners had been drawn to the windows by the commotion, they now withdrew. The taxi rank was empty. The security guards had disappeared from their posts. If any cars drove past, they did not stop.

It was Bocão who called Yvonne. After the disturbance that afternoon she had given them coins for the telephone in case of trouble. '*Tia, Tia!*' he shouted down the phone, 'They've been killing us all. The *extermínio, Tia!*'[3]

Yvonne did not even pause to wake her sleeping husband and tell him where she was going. She ran to her car and drove. By the time she arrived, the Civil Police were there. Rogeirinho had run to the police station on Praça Mauá to fetch them. The media had already been tipped off. The church forecourt flashed with police and camera lights. Fifty-odd hysterical children trembled and wailed. Journalists moved around the bodies, filming and photographing them.

The children launched themselves at Yvonne, clamouring for her, reaching out with dozens of arms from the blankets that they had wrapped around themselves. She found herself being pulled down onto the pavement. They clung to her from all sides with their arms around her limbs, her waist, her neck. Cameras flashed all around them. The following week, *Veja*, Brazil's most widely circulated news weekly, would carry a picture of Yvonne's distress, one white face at the centre of a mass of grey blankets and black curls.

The mortuary van arrived and the police picked up the bodies by the ankles and the armpits and slung them into the open caskets in the back of the vehicle. The van drove off. The police drove off. The journalists drove off. The bystanders dispersed. It was now around 3.00 or 4.00 in the morning. Yvonne and the children sat, and the children told her again and again what had happened.

The sky over Rio began to lighten. The hum of cars and buses and the squeaking of brakes rose to the windows of the high-rises, singing in the dawn. Car horns sounded, trolley wheels rolled over the cobbles, voices called out greetings and birds chattered. Air conditioning units dripped gently onto the pavement. All around the city, chairs were dragged into place in front of shop doors or fruit sellers' carts or newspaper kiosks. The *Cariocas* set themselves up and sat themselves down. The streets began to fill with people going to work. The sun rose and cast the sharp shadows of palm trees over barefooted people lying on cardboard in parks bordering the sea. The water sparkled in the bays, and all around, like sedated watchdogs, the hills slumbered.

Eventually a Civil Police car drifted over to Candelária. A couple of policemen got out. They suggested to Yvonne that it might not be such a bad idea if she brought the children over to the police station so that they could take some statements.

PART II

Investigations

7

Identification Parades

'THAT MORNING,' WROTE one newspaper commentator, 'arrived like a punch in the city's stomach.'[4] Marjorie turned on her radio to the news. Marcelo was shaken awake by his mother to ask him if Candelária was where he worked. Andrea, whose husband had heard but did not dare tell her, was taking a boy to a hospital appointment when he mentioned it. She left him at the hospital and ran to the church.

Five children had been murdered around Candelária, but the area was not sealed off. At the church there was a mass of people. Hundreds of curious bystanders milled around and the media was out in force. This was what Marcelo retained more than anything from that morning: the sheer number of people. Cristina was already there, dividing up the tasks. She and Andrea would go to the police station, Marcelo and Marjorie to the morgue. Already the two crimes – the killings at Candelária and the killings at the Aterro do Flamengo which Wagner had survived – were assumed to be linked. Cristina sent other *Centro Brasileiro* workers to the hospital to seek information about Come-Gato and Wagner.

At the morgue, one of the employees waved Marcelo and Marjorie in: 'The bodies are in there. Take a look if you want.'

'There was no form of registration. I wasn't asked to identify myself,' recalled Marcelo. He could not remember Marjorie being there. All he could remember was a room full of bodies: indigents, victims of other crimes, bodies pulled from the water. They went among them looking for any children they might recognise. But so many of the children in that huge group had been recent arrivals, 'Apart from Come-Gato,' said Marjorie, 'our relationship with the others who died was fleeting.' Marcelo recognised one boy. He remembered his name, because it was the same as his own: Marcelo. They had played football together on the night of the party. Marjorie did not trust her memory: 'I remember their physiognomy as if they were frozen in terror.' She raised her arm in front of her, stiffly, as if warding something off. 'I remember seeing a hand like that. I don't know if perhaps the shock so was great, that everything was so intense that I...' she tailed off and shook the thought free. 'But I don't think so.' She tried to reassure herself. 'I think that, depending on the situation, a person is slack. But anyway, it was very grotesque.'

Yvonne was at the police station with the children. She had ferried them in small groups over to Praça Mauá in her own car. It was chaos. The fifty-odd Candelária children had been joined by terrified street children from all over the city centre who wanted to be taken off the streets. They had wrapped T-shirts around their heads to mask their faces. Within hours, the rumour began to circulate that members of the rival Cinelândia group of street kids were being paid to pass themselves off as survivors and give false statements. Rio lived and breathed conspiracy theories. This would only be the first of many in the Candelária case.

In Brazil there was no culture of investigative policing. The Civil Police were as badly paid, under-trained, under-valued and under-resourced as their military colleagues, but better educated, so not quite as despised. A *Delegado* must have a university degree, and was addressed as 'Doctor', but his registrar still bashed away on a manual typewriter to record statements and brought his own toilet paper in to work. When charges were brought and prosecutions pursued, it was on the basis of eyewitness evidence and confessions, which might sometimes be obtained from criminal suspects by the simple method of torture.

So there had been no rigorous examination of either the crime scenes at Candelária or at Flamengo where Paulo and Gambazinho had been shot, in fact, neither scene had even been sealed off. Some bullet cases had been gathered up, some photos taken, but the kind of detailed, painstaking work of minute examination of the scene and bodies, which might have revealed important information about the killers – such as how many there had been, their height, whether they were right- or left-handed – was outside the experience of the Brazilian police. And because the areas had not been sealed off, anyone outside the group of children who might have seen something had simply slipped away, and there was no tradition of intensive door-to-door enquiry to follow up on who might have been working there that night.

Post-mortems were equally cursory. The forensic institutes were attached to the Military Police, so there was already a disincentive to be over-zealous about finding evidence in cases of *extermínio* killings, even if the capacity to do so had existed. The forensic pathologists were given scope to do little more than to remove bullets* and record entry and exit wounds. Traditionally, autopsy reports would reach the conclusion that

---

* Sometimes bullets were missed. When the remains of survivors of another Rio massacre (that of Vigário Geral) were removed for reburial in 1996, bullets were found in the coffins.

the victim was dead from a bullet wound, but that there was insufficient evidence to deduce homicide.

In the Candelária case, all the Civil Police had was twelve bullets, a handful of bullet cases and a group of traumatised, dysfunctional children who had been left to sit around all night contaminating each others' fragile testimonies. And they had Wagner. Wagner lay in hospital, barely able to lift his head from the pillow, his face only partially visible beneath swaths of bandages, his voice reedy and strained. He had a visit from the *Delegado* assigned to the case, Dr Wilson Machado Velho, who brought a police artist with him. 'Be careful,' he said to Wagner. 'You don't want to put an innocent man in jail.'

In a television statement, Military Police Colonel Farias half-heartedly denied that there was any evidence to suggest the involvement of Military Police. But if no one asked 'Why?' it happened, no one asked 'Who?' in the more general sense, either. In Brazil the bogeyman was not a figment of anyone's imagination. It was the *extermínio*, and everyone knew that the *extermínio* was the preserve of the Military Police, with only the occasional participation of civilians or Civil Police. The question 'Who?' was a matter of detail only. The children had said it was police, and, as Wagner said, 'In Brazil you know who's police. Who's military. Who's civil. It's not like in Europe. In Brazil you *know*.' In fact, the Military Police had already assigned the equivalent of an internal investigation team to assist the Civil Police inquiry, under the leadership of Colonel Valmir Alves Brum.

Brum had just the right face for a maverick detective: good-looking in a craggy, world-weary way. He rarely smiled and kept his distance behind a slightly irritable, old-fashioned formality.

Inevitably, he was not popular with most of his colleagues but he loved his work. 'I come from humble origins. I was born into a poor family.' He laughed, 'I'm still poor today! My origins are in that poverty that still exists, which is the Baixada Fluminense. I was brought up in a neighbourhood called Mesquita. My whole family is still there. When I was growing up, people asked, "Where's the body today?" So I saw a lot of killing there. I don't know if that influenced my profession.

'My first job was as a primary school teacher. Then one day I found out that the Military Police was holding an entrance exam. I passed – in thirteenth place. I stayed in thirteenth place throughout the three years at the police academy!

'When I left the academy the Military Police didn't work in investigations. But I started to work in certain places where investigation was being done and I discovered that I liked it. I never stopped. My first job was the death of a student who'd been shot by Fifth Battalion Military Police with the involvement of the battalion commander. I investigated it, found out what happened for the family. The commander was convicted. But from then on my life became hell. I was punished. Because how can a lieutenant investigate a police colonel? And from then on I've specialised in investigating homicides.'

Every so often someone found a way to fire him. How many times? 'Hmmm,' He had to pause to think. 'Really *seriously*...' He listed them off to himself. According to his count, he was currently on his fifth suspension from duty. It was amazing that he had ever risen to the rank of Colonel.

'I got here because at the time that I was rising through the ranks the institution was led by someone with social vision, with a human rights vision, Colonel Carlos Magno Cerqueira. He was killed by those criminals too,' he added gloomily, referring to the organised criminal element in the Military Police that he regarded as 'his enemies'. 'He was assassinated by a policeman in 1999.'

Even for someone as hardened to murder as Colonel Brum, the Candelária case was shocking. It was not so much the event itself as the reaction to it. Four of the eight boys killed had been under fifteen. The youngest to die, Pimpolho, was only eleven. But many *Cariocas* were unmoved by their youth. One of the first steps the investigating police took was to set up a hotline number. They received a large number of calls, but no one was using it to impart information: 'The message was: "They were right to kill them; they should kill all of them." I was horrified to discover that society was more cruel than you could imagine.

'These extermination groups arise from neglect, sometimes, because both the people and the police are in the streets. The police think that if they don't do something nobody will do anything. That's certainly what happened in Candelária, because those vulnerable children and adolescents were a disturbance to the church, to the bankers, to the businesses, to the pedestrians, to the police. People thought of it as a decontamination.'

Many may have seen the massacre as a clean-up operation, but the massacre divided public opinion, and there was enough outrage for there to be enormous pressure on the police to produce a result. It was one thing for anonymous children to disappear, but it was quite another for a mass murder to be carried out in the centre of town and in front of a church. People worried that it was deliberate, that the *extermínio* was sending a message to the city that it was raising the stakes. And for some years Brazil had been receiving harsh criticism about its treatment of street children, and there was a national sensitivity about the country's international image. Candelária was another embarrassment for Brazil, and so there was sufficient political will in enough areas of influence to give the case a high political profile. The word on everyone's lips was 'impunity', for which Brazil was infamous. Everyone expected Candelária to end in impunity.

When the ballistics reports came back, they confirmed what had already been assumed: that the shooting of Wagner, Paulo and Gambazinho had been linked to the events at Candelária. One gun had been used at both locations. The ballistics also showed that a minimum of four guns had been used between the two sites.

In the meantime, they had been interviewing the street kids, who were inevitably wildly inconsistent. 'You can never take a child's statement too seriously,' said Brum, 'because they don't see things in the same way as an adult. They're not selective.' However, some details emerged as being significant. Many of the kids spoke of the presence of two cars at the scene, which suggested the involvement of up to eight men. And many of them referred to the stone-throwing incident, Neilton's arrest and the threat that they had received the day before from the traffic police.

The obvious place to start the investigation was with the men who policed the area. Extermination squads tended to be territorial. It was the Fifth Battalion who were being made to look bad if Candelária was out of control. All official weapons in the Fifth Battalion were confiscated and tested. It was no great surprise when nothing came back. Police only used official weapons during official operations. They had their own guns for unofficial killings.

Based on the children's descriptions, around forty members of the battalion were also brought in for identity parades. The way in which these identity parades were conducted would have enormous significance for the outcome of the case. Journalist Octavio Guedes later recalled in a television interview that the police station 'was like a cauldron'.[5] The holding cells in many Brazilian stations were de facto remand prisons; crime was high and justice slow and detainees might spend years sharing a large cell with dozens of other men. As the Military Police were brought in to be put in the line-ups, there was a chanting of 'Murderers! Murderers!' from the holding cells. The kids were brought in, wrapped in blankets, through a cordon of television cameras. 'The whole thing had a carnival atmosphere,' said Octavio Guedes.[6]

The line-ups were not governed by the kind of stringent rules that exist in some countries. In the UK, for example, a line-up must include eight to twelve people of similar physical appearance – height, colouring, ethnic background, age. They must also be of a similar station in life, so that the witness is not influenced by the myriad subconscious class signals that are given off by dress, manner and hairstyle. The suspect is allowed to object to any of the people in the line and may move position between identifications.

The Candelária line-ups were a rather looser affair. Groups of policemen from the Fifth Battalion of all different ages, shapes, sizes and colours were put in front of the glass. Some random 'extras' were brought in from the Civil Police and the media scrum and the kids were invited to point at anyone they recognised. Inevitably, civilians were pointed out, including a TV cameraman. Some of the kids later admitted to being high on glue at the time of the identifications.

The identifications produced four suspects. The first was Marcos Vinícius Borges Emmanuel, the traffic policeman who had arrested Neilton. He was easy to pick out. After all, the kids had seen him the day before the massacre, but did that mean that he had been with the extermination squad? He did not fit the profile of a death squad member. At twenty-six, he was a boyish-looking white man who appeared as if his bottom lip might give way at any moment. One of his grandmothers came from France, which was enough to confer respectability on the entire family, which swore that Emmanuel had been at home on the night of the massacre. Emmanuel was also picked out by Wagner, who, two days after his shooting, was hoisted into the back of a van, stiff and contorted in a wheelchair, to be driven to the police station.

Another unlikely killer was an unassuming devout Evangelical Christian, Cláudio Luiz Andrade dos Santos, who was identified by several of the children. The kids' statements had been consistent about the presence of a black man among the killers, and they had also mentioned two members of the Fifth Battalion who were notorious among the street population for brutality. Their nicknames were 'Pelé', a common nickname for black people in Brazil, for obvious reasons, and 'Xuxa' – another common nickname for darker-skinned people, used ironically after a blonde television star. Both Pelé and Xuxa were brought in, but not picked out by any of the witnesses. However, there was also a plain-clothes arm of the battalion, and Brum put a call through to its commander to ask if there were any black people among them. The commander said that there were two, himself and Cláudio. Cláudio was at home when he received a phone call requesting him to go in (the commander himself was not asked to appear). He was put in a line-up with men who were all lighter skinned than himself, and picked out.

Initially, Brum had his doubts about both Emmanuel and Cláudio, especially the latter: 'I was almost certain that he had not been involved,' he said.

Two other men who were identified by the witnesses appeared to make more sense. One, Jurandir Gomes da França, was not a policeman, but a locksmith. He had been brought in because he was 'Xuxa's' cousin and had been in the area the previous night. And finally, there was Lieutenant Marcelo Ferreira Cortes. He was a good fit for one of the descriptions that Wagner had given the police artist – right down to the chip in his front tooth. It was Wagner alone who picked him out of the line-ups. But Cortes had what appeared to be a compelling alibi. When Wagner collapsed at the garage, the attendant had called the police. Cortes was not on duty at the time, but he was back at the barracks when the call came through, and had volunteered to accompany his colleague. Cortes claimed that he was the one who administered first aid to Wagner and who was talking to him while he was waiting for the ambulance. Brum did not dispute his version of events, but it did not preclude Cortes from having participated in the massacre *and* having answered the call when he realised that there had been a survivor. It was sometimes a practice of police who had carried out shootings to accompany their victims to hospital to throw off suspicion.

The investigating officers were working on the principle that the killings had been part of a drunken, drug-fuelled spree, and both Jurandir and Cortes had been in town that night, 'doing I don't know what,' according to Brum. When pressed to admit that he did know what, he said delicately – he always chose his words extremely carefully – that 'they had been conducting an erotic tour of the city'. The papers were not so shy: 'Orgy with Women Before Killing' shouted one headline.[7]

The investigating officers were convinced that there were more people involved, but for now they had four eyewitness identifications to work with and they immediately secured detention orders for all four suspects. The Civil Police Chief, Nilo Batista, expressed his satisfaction to the press and declared the case solved. The arrests seemed like a small but significant victory for the human rights contingent, which was so busy trying to ensure that the case survived the long road to trial, that it did not really question that it had all been uncharacteristically straightforward. It was only in hindsight that this looked a little odd. As journalist Octavio Guedes put it years later: 'We went to bed in the country of impunity, and we woke up on the Monday in the country of police efficiency.'[8]

8

Hospitals and Funerals

YVONNE AND CRISTINA had met only a week before but they both understood one thing with great clarity: that the journalists would soon move on to the next big story, and that if they could not hold the interest of the media, the case would never come to trial. Each of the women was strong-willed, stubborn, persistent and thick-skinned. Under normal circumstances they would have veered away from each other like magnets set on opposing poles. However, they both cared deeply that the Candelária murders should not go unpunished, and that this tragedy should serve to highlight the need for a coherent policy regarding Rio's street population. For that to be possible, they knew instinctively that it would require a lot of noise. And to make noise, they needed each other.

Yvonne sat herself down on the steps of Candelária with a placard, which proclaimed: 'Two days since the Candelária massacre', 'Three days since the Candelária massacre', and so on. Yvonne was photogenic, articulate in several languages and played the role of the 'Angel of Candelária' very well. The press lapped her up. Cristina made phone calls, sent faxes, knocked on doors and made a point of turning up wherever she was least wanted.

The most immediate problem was what to do with all those children. The state government made a building available called CERIM, an acronym which would soon be defunct and the words it stood for forgotten. The building, which had recently been built for an orphanage, or something along those lines, stood empty. It had beds and showers, and they quickly staffed it with employees from state institutions, such as from the FUNABEM system. 'It was crazy!' said Andrea. 'Employees from institutions! A kid who lives on the streets lives outside any system of rules.' Technically, the children were now the state's responsibility, and the *Centro Brasileiro* had no place in their care, but that was not how Andrea understood it. At the police station the children had clung to the *Centro Brasileiro* caseworkers and refused to let them go. They went with them to CERIM. The CERIM employees, understandably, did not want them there. 'We said we had an ethical commitment to these children, and that they could say what they liked, we weren't leaving. All the other non-governmental organisations [NGOs] said that we should leave, that it was the responsibility of the state and not of NGOs. What equivocation! We committed to stay and they believed that we were being irresponsible.' The *Centro Brasileiro* asked for a shift system of caseworkers with experience of working with street children to be set up, but no one else wanted to be involved. Instead, Andrea and Marjorie persuaded their husbands to come and sleep at CERIM with them.

'The kids didn't sleep,' said Andrea. 'They started to sleep, then they woke up screaming. They had nightmares the whole time. They began to imagine that they were going to be exterminated as a whole group inside CERIM.'

'There was a huge movement of people: the police, the press, the families. Lots of people coming in and out,' remembered Marcelo. 'And it was there that the fear started, because the children were frightened, we were frightened. CERIM was a place of fear.'

There was a rumour circulating that the names of all the *Centro Brasileiro* caseworkers were on a death list. One day Andrea took some of the kids out in the *Centro Brasileiro* van because they were concerned about four of their friends who had not been seen since the night of the massacre. They wanted to go to the city centre to look for them. The van, which displayed the *Centro Brasileiro* logo, was pulled over by an unmarked police car. 'As they [the police] were getting out of the car the kids, who were hiding in the back of the van with their T-shirts covering their faces, were whispering, "It's them! It's them!" The policeman said, "You have to follow us to the battalion." A car parked in front of our van, and another behind. At that very moment a state deputy★ who was accompanying the case drove past. She saw the van, recognised it and stopped. The police left, and she escorted us back to CERIM.'

The time for utopian dreams was over. It was not that the caseworkers had not had some sense of danger – the issue of violence against street children had been very prominent since the end of the dictatorship – but, as Marcelo said, 'We *talked* about it, theoretically, but we'd never come across it first-hand.' It was generally the poor who suffered from the violence; the caseworkers had felt protected by their class and education. But after the massacre, said Marcelo, 'It seemed that I'd encountered a monster. A murderous monster. The dark forces came out and

---

★ A popularly elected member of the state legislative assembly.

demonstrated that it wasn't as we had thought. If you wanted to do something to change the life of those people, you risked your life too. That had never crossed our minds before.'

Three days after the massacre the funerals began. First to be buried were the two youngest, Pimpolho and Careca. Their mothers had come down from the hills to identify them as Paulo Roberto de Oliveira and Marcelo Cândido de Jesus, and their bodies were released from the morgue. The funerals took place in the white-walled Caju cemetery, a maze of stone vaults overlooked by mournful angels and filled with the sound of traffic from the Avenida Brasil. The kids were bussed in and emerged with their wrapped T-shirts around their heads to hide their faces. It was a manifestation of their fear, but the effect recalled images of prison rioters and hostage-takers and only served to consolidate the idea of the children as dangerous criminals. Only the irrepressible Beth made no attempt to disguise herself, but leant out of the bus window and furiously shouted her accusations to the assembled microphones. The kids were filmed descending from the bus. An arm stretched out to help Andrea down. Her face, which normally danced with smiles, was stricken, her eyes dark. The press crouched above the strange funeral procession, lined up on the high walls of the cemetery like gargoyles.

It seemed to the *Centro Brasileiro* that suddenly the whole of Rio claimed to have been working with the Candelária group. All sorts of people that they had never heard of were taking advantage of the photo opportunity that Candelária offered – politicians made statements to the press; other NGOs, sniffing international fund-raising opportunities in the air, sent representatives to the funerals. Many were simply offering support, but Marcelo found them all bizarre and threatening: 'Anyone I didn't know who appeared at that time I found strange, especially when someone turned up who said that they'd known the kids for X amount of time – a whole load of people appeared saying that they'd known them, that they'd done this, that they'd done that. So the general feeling was that all these people who suddenly appeared had bad motives. I felt estranged from them, believing that many of them were taking advantage, and were using the situation to boost their profiles. Because the massacre unleashed an international machine, a political machine, an enormous social machine. All of them claimed to have been intimates; all of them said that they'd been fighting for those children. The authorities had been fighting – everyone had been doing something to try to prevent it from happening.'

The children carried banners with the names of the dead through the centre of the cemetery, and shouted them out: 'Careca!' '*Presente*!' 'Pimpolho!' '*Presente*!' The funeral service in the little chapel was disrupted by a group of street kids from the rival Cinelândia group. They attacked journalists and damaged the windows. And so Pimpolho and Careca's sad brief lives were forgotten, even at their own funerals, as the press crowded in to secure images of street kids smashing up the church.

The following day Come-Gato, who never came out of his coma, died in hospital. His parents, who had turned him away only two weeks before, came to identify his body. One by one the bodies were claimed and interred, pushed into simple vaults in the walls of Caju cemetery. Finally, only Gambazinho remained unidentified. None of the kids knew his real name – they only ever called each other by their nicknames. He had been in FUNABEM and Wagner remembered him from the orphanage. He had not liked school and often ran away. 'He was always being disciplined. But he played football. He played well. He played music and was in the band with me. But he was very rebellious – the rebelliousness of children.' What paperwork had existed on Gambazinho had been lost, and with it, any proof of his existence. He was interred, and, on the cross which stood in front of Candelária, he was remembered between quotation marks: 'Gambazinho'.

For the first time since he had entered the orphanage fifteen years before, Wagner was completely alone. He occupied a private room in the Hospital Souza Aguiar with a police guard on the door. There was nothing in the room except blank walls and silence. 'I didn't even have a toothbrush!' One day Brum turned up at the hospital to interview Wagner and found that one of his police guards had just popped off to have a coffee. He transferred responsibility for Wagner's security to another battalion, the Special Operations Batallion, BOPE. 'They had their problems, but they treated me only with respect. One of them even brought in a radio to give to me.'

Wagner did not know it, but Cristina was trying to contact him. The Brazilian legal system provided for victims or their families to have their interests represented throughout the legal process by a 'Prosecution Assistant'. This assistant was not appointed by the court, but by the victim, and was permitted an auxiliary role to the court-appointed public prosecutors. 'No one had any contact with Wagner,' said Cristina. She feared that they were isolating him – the only survivor – in order to 'brainwash' him and prevent him from making certain identifications. 'When there were identification line-ups we all met, but the police were with Wagner, so we were on one side, and Wagner was on the other. So I started to give Dr Machado notes to pass on to Wagner, saying, "Wagner, you need a lawyer." But the notes never reached him.'

Wagner was recovering well, considering he had been shot twice in the face and once in the chest. The bullet to his torso had exited without damage to any internal organs, and surgeons had been able to remove another bullet from his face. However, it was too risky to remove a third bullet, which was still lodged in the back of his neck. Apart from a couple of scars and a look of slight incomprehension, captured on camera by an American journalist who had taken interest in him, he looked just like his old self. And, despite his dazed expression, he was very clear about what he wanted. 'I didn't have a father and mother, but I had people who taught me. I'd always suffered a lot since I was a child. I'm not the sort of person who settles for injustice, and because I'd suffered a lot since I was a child I could always see what was right. So I decided that even if I died for it, I was going to testify, because they [the police] took away their right to life, and they did it in a cowardly way.'

At CERIM the *Centro Brasileiro* workers and Yvonne had their hands full, trying to reassure the kids. There was a huge amount of coming and going, what with funerals and identifications and hearings. The Seventh Day Mass was held at Candelária to remember the victims. The kids had never been inside the church before. They gazed up at the gold of the vaulted ceiling, and dizzied themselves under the dome. In the alcoves, painted saints bled from their wounds. One after the other, dignitaries spoke at the lecterns, supported by the wings of enormous carved angels. But the children were not impressed. They had discerned that no one had spoken of them. They expressed their disillusionment to Yvonne. They could not understand how they had been forgotten so quickly, when they were also victims of this tragedy, when they were the ones who were both bereaved and terrified.

After a couple of weeks at CERIM the question arose as to where the kids would go next. CERIM was only a temporary measure. If the children's families could not be located, they would have to be distributed around various established units. The investigation had narrowed the witnesses down to a small group, which included Beth and Rogeirinho. As for the rest, they were now simply abandoned children, like any others.

The authorities resolved to split the children up between a number of units known as CRIAMs, which were juvenile detention units. On the whole, the children had not been convicted as young offenders, and certainly did not think of themselves as such. They perceived the idea of sending them to a CRIAM as simply unfair, in that terrible absolute way in which children understand fairness. They also did not want to be split up. In the few weeks in which they had been together they had forged a strong sense of togetherness, the family fantasy was still being played out. The idea of separation compounded their fears. When, early one morning, the vans turned up to take them away in different directions, the kids rioted.

The *Centro Brasileiro* workers, attempting to grab flailing, hysterical children as they hurled chairs across the rooms, felt let down by the authorities. The kids were dragged kicking and screaming to the vans and were driven off to the CRIAMS, where over the next few days they would run away in ones and twos and threes, to drift back up into the hills or back down onto the streets.

'The state lost a big opportunity to set up a project with those kids,' said Cristina. 'All of Rio's street kids felt vulnerable and unprotected and wanted to go to CERIM. And the state did not understand that it was a delicate situation, that they could have found out who they were, that they could have worked with them, that they had most of Rio's street kids in their hands.'

Another solution had been found for the seven witnesses. Brazil was new to the idea of witness protection and the Rio government improvised by setting up a witness house in an old government building, an initiative of which they were so proud that they announced its inauguration to the press. Everyone knew where it was, which was right in the city centre. It was a low building with small, barred windows set behind a high white wall and a solid metal gate. No one seemed able to say for what purpose the building had been used before, but it looked like something that had been left over from the military regime – the kind of place into which people disappeared to be tortured.

When Wagner was well enough he was transferred to the witness house. The other Candelária witnesses were already there. 'It was worse than living on the streets,' said Wagner. It was a barren place. He slept on a mattress on the floor, without so much as a pillow. Often the food arrived smelling of putrefaction. There was absolutely nothing to do. But it was not a prison, as the authorities were at pains to point out. And it was not a witness protection programme, either. There was no mutually binding contract which demanded discretion in exchange for security. It was more like a hostel for witnesses, and they came and went freely. The Candelária witnesses would disappear for a few days and return when they were hungry or scared. People dropped by. Neilton, who had passed on the threat on the night of the massacre, visited the witness house for a chat. He was not going to be stupid enough to testify. He said he was off to São Paulo, and that was the last that Wagner saw of him.

The streets around the witness house attracted the poor. Beggars sat in the gutters, prostitutes stood on the street corners. The witnesses always had plenty of food, disgusting though it often was, and they began to give it away. The beggars began to queue at the witness house door. Wagner befriended one family across the road and took them food every day. The house began to fill up with witnesses from other cases. They went out on the town together at night in large groups.

'Didn't anyone suggest that it wasn't such a good idea for you to all go out together, or ... perhaps ... at all?'

Wagner shrugged and sucked his teeth. 'It wasn't a prison! I was a grown-up!' Still, he must have felt some constraint, because he often said 'when I was in prison' when he was referring to his time at the witness house.

Part of this constraint came from within himself. He had always, he said, wanted to be a 'good little boy'. There was always a tension in his life between wanting to do what was right, and wanting to be where there was movement and noise and music. Wagner was different from the other Candelária witnesses. Nothing dented his determination to testify. He had not had much to do with any of the other kids before the massacre, but at the witness house they talked. 'For them it was: "They died. The police killed them." They didn't have an understanding of what a human life is. And deep down they were certain of one thing, no matter how much they testified: nothing would result from it. They weren't going to be heard or acknowledged. They would just suffer more.'

9

Whispers and Rumours

THE CANDELÁRIA CASE fell to two young public prosecutors: José Muiños Piñeiro Filho and Maurício Assayag. The court allocated cases by lottery, so, in a sense, they 'won' the case. It was too early to say whether this was good or bad luck, but they were conscious of the symbolic importance of Candelária.

Piñeiro was a good storyteller, which was clearly one of the reasons that he was highly respected in his profession. It was he who had had to extract, from the mountains of papers and from the whisperings of rumour and intrigue, a clear version of events that would be persuasive to a jury. In 1993, Yvonne had been impressed and reassured by his energy and enthusiasm. He still had both fourteen years later, and Candelária was still a good story.

'What was surprising at the time was that this kind of killing happened in the Baixada Fluminense, on the periphery of Rio de Janeiro. It wasn't common in the centre of the city. All of a sudden, Rio de Janeiro, the cultural capital of the country, saw itself stained by the death of eight children in the financial centre of the city, in front of the historical Church of Candelária! It was as if it were a message to society. I would say that the Candelária massacre is a historical turning point. Why? Because it woke up Brazilian society to a phenomenon which was occurring in the periphery. That is to say, the extermination of children who were poor, and didn't have the protection of the state. But it occurred far away. Now it had occurred on our streets. That was a turning point, and it changed our society. Evidently, it was shocking. It didn't just stain Rio's history, but the history of the state, the history of the country, and it had international repercussions. Perhaps it was the first time that a criminal case in Brazil had this repercussion.'

When Piñeiro and Assayag came to the case, four or five days after the massacre, the four men were already under arrest. 'I'll sum up the three initial problems. The first was to ensure that the kids could make more reliable statements, because what with their excitability, the conditions of the incident … it was in the early hours of the morning, they were sleeping … You need to have very solid evidence. There was a lot of contradiction between them, which is only natural. So there were difficulties in getting the more reliable and consistent statements. We had to filter them.

'The second problem was that these kids should have shelter and that's why I say that it was a turning point, because the witness protection issue that we have in Brazil today has its origin in the Candelária case.

'Third was the motivation for the crime. What was it that caused eight children to be killed in those conditions, at that time, in that cowardly manner? Immediately there was a version that wasn't given much credence. The events occurred at night, but at 5.00 in the afternoon there had been a problem. A traffic policeman saw a minor with a tin of glue, which is not considered a drug in our legislation. He confiscated the tin and arrested the minor. But in arresting him stones were thrown and a vehicle was hit. Later this minor was released, because it was not an illicit practice. But it was difficult for people to accept this. No! Because of that? Carry out a massacre because of a minor's rebellion, which is sadly a common occurrence – no. It must be something more serious.'

The investigation pursued various rumours. 'First: two days before, in a street nearby, a group of minors was carrying out thefts and set fire to a shop. The shopkeeper could have acted in revenge. Second: in that locality there are a lot of illegal bookies★ and, obviously, these kids were causing trouble because they were there doing nothing, carrying out thefts, the bookies might have ordered them to be killed, because there had already been threats. Third: Candelária businesses, which were being disrupted. Apart from these, there was a notable case. A week before, a lady had been killed nearby when she was run over. She had been mugged by two boys, ran, and ended up being hit by a bus. Her husband was an ex-army officer, and there was talk at the time that he was beside himself. So the police were investigating because he might have contracted someone to kill them. These and other angles were being investigated. And each time, it was a hypothesis, but it didn't fit, it wasn't confirmed. On the contrary. It was the first reason: police being attacked, insulted in public.'

But this was Rio. It could not be as simple as that. Yvonne for one was dismissive of the 'stone as catalyst' theory. 'The children threw stones at cars every day,' she said. She had another theory. She said that Come-Gato dealt drugs to the children on

---

★ The *Jogo do Bicho* is an illegal lottery played on every street corner in Rio de Janeiro. The game has been linked to organised crime.

behalf of a policeman. 'I knew that the drugs were hidden in the fountain. After the massacre I took the kids to the police station and then before I went home to change my clothes, I thought: the drugs in the fountain! If they find them it's all over. So I went there, got into the fountain, and pulled out a bag of cannabis. Then I went to Praça Quinze and threw it into the sea. What must have happened was some kind of non-payment. And the police, they went there to kill one person, not to carry out a massacre.' Having shot Wagner and the others, and then their intended target, Come-Gato, they were 'on a roll'. All those kids running: 'It's the extermination squad mentality: "Let's clean up."'

Andrea had a completely different theory. She was not so concerned with who had carried out the killings, but became, in her own word, 'obsessed' with knowing who gave the order: 'I don't think it was an extermination of street kids. I think that this extermination was to clean Rio de Janeiro of gays and transvestites, of this filth. It was a big issue in the twentieth century. Now it has diminished because gay rights protection is very strong. It was combined with the question of AIDS and the preoccupation that they were the main contaminators.'

The story that Wagner heard was that the house of one of the policemen had been robbed by someone light-skinned, someone who looked like Come-Gato. But that made no sense to him, 'Come-Gato wouldn't have known where their houses were.' In any case, Wagner did not torture himself trying to understand their motives. It was simply that immutable force, evil: 'The truth is that what happened happens every day in Rio. It's cultural and social prejudice. That's why it happened. It was a revolt, a cleaning operation. The guys saw what was going on there. That they mugged people, everyone knew. On that day the guys were coked up – they'd snorted a lot, drunk a lot. And they wanted an adventure, to carry out evil. That's their instinct. It even makes sense that it was because of the stone, because he [Emmanuel] was pissed off. I believe that what was more demoralising for him was that the person that he arrested wasn't detained. That messed with his ego. There's no logic to it. The logic is that the guys were pissed off. The kids were messing around there. And one day they decided to give it a clean sweep.'

Wagner's perception, having seen the police from the streets, was closest to Brum's, who knew the police from within. It was at the police station that the final affront took place, not at the moment of throwing the stone. Emmanuel, said Brum, had 'acted on his own initiative and arrested this adolescent and took him to the First Police Station in Praça Mauá. The *Delegado* looked, made an analysis and saw that there was not much legal basis for detaining them.' The kids 'attacked a policeman and this resulted in a patrol vehicle being damaged by a stone and caused serious discontent in the region. It was because of that. Today I know that that's what it was. At the time I had no idea.'

'Was it really just because of that? Did he have such an acute sense of honour?'

Brum was irritated at the over-simplification. 'It was *just* because of that! It's not a sense of honour. They thought that if they didn't do something, no one would do anything. Perhaps the greater motive was the *Delegado's* disrespect in not dealing with the case when he was taken to the police station. Glue is not considered a drug, so he acted according to the law. But in reality he should have referred the child to the minors' police station for a socio-educational measure.'

'So why were they looking for Ruço?'

'Because Ruço was the leader of the group. Emmanuel knew that. He was the leader of the group and he had to be punished in an exemplary way.'

It all kept coming back to Emmanuel, unlikely a candidate as he appeared: 'Of French origin, well-educated,' was how Piñeiro described him. 'A person with an unusual family for someone entering the Military Police, who are normally people with greater needs. Who even had French citizenship. He was put up for identification, was recognised by various minors, and even by Wagner. And he was detained and stayed in detention. He denied everything absolutely, as did all of the others who were taken for identification and eventually identified. But we got down to work.'

10

Vigário Geral

AND THEN, ON 29 August 1993, little more than a month after the Candelária massacre, the next big story happened.

The *favela* of Vigário Geral was notorious for having been the headquarters of the Red Command, Rio's oldest drug faction. Vigário Geral was fortified by a high wall which ran alongside the railway line, and access to it was by way of a narrow footbridge. There was a way in by road, but that ran through enemy faction territory in the *favela* of Parada de Lucas, so Vigário Geral felt self-contained and cut off. Visitors met their hosts by the footbridge and were escorted across and down the steps, visible to anyone watching out for strangers.

On the night of 19 August, a group of men sat in a bar playing cards. They heard some distant shots, but thought little of it. They were workers and whatever it was had nothing to do with them. At around 11.30 a couple of policemen came into the bar and demanded papers. One of the men was explaining that they were all workers when someone threw a hand grenade. The explosion was followed by shooting. One man escaped through the back door. Everyone else in the bar was killed apart from one man, Jadir, who lay under the body of his friend, bleeding from five bullet wounds and listening. The shooting was not confined to the bar. He could hear it in the streets. He could hear it coming from the house of 'the believers.'[9]

In 13 Antônio Mendes Street, the family of Gilberto Cardoso dos Santos were settling down to bed. They were known in Vigário Geral for being devout evangelical Christians. In the house was Gilberto's wife, Jane, four of their five daughters, their son and daughter-in-law and five grandchildren. The killers debated whether or not to kill the grandchildren, and decided against it. The oldest granddaughter grabbed the six-week-old baby and the children left via a window. Everyone else in the house was killed. Fifteen-year-old Luciene still lay on the sofa, where she had been sleeping. Jane died clutching her Bible.[10]

When the shooting stopped, twenty-one people were dead. The killers were police. They belonged to a death squad calling itself the *Cavalos Corredores* – Running Horses. Over thirty men had participated in the shooting spree. It was a revenge attack, a deeply murky story of the Vigário Geral *tráfico* falling out with police over kickbacks on cocaine shipments. The day before, the *tráfico* had killed four policemen who were somewhere they should not have been.

The massacre stunned Rio. Not one of the twenty-one people killed had anything to do with drug trafficking. Their bodies were displayed in two rows of open caskets, stiff and contorted in the simple wooden boxes, and surrounded by Vigário Geral residents, in an image which was widely published throughout the world's press. It was an image so strong that Marcelo suspected that it had super-imposed itself upon his memory of what he had seen in the morgue after the Candelária massacre.

Candelária had been seen by many *Cariocas* as a decontamination, but this was different. The victims had work papers, went to church. They were widely acknowledged to belong to the category of 'innocents'. Something was wrong with Rio. The juxtaposition of the two massacres would have consequences for the outcome of the Candelária case. In some ways Vigário Geral would eclipse Candelária and divert time, energy and resources away from it. But it also meant that the two events became associated with the same malaise and with the spontaneous reaction against it. At last, it seemed, Rio de Janeiro had been shaken awake.

The awakening took the form of a movement which would eventually become known as 'Viva Rio'. It started as little more than a desire to do something in answer to the escalating violence which had culminated in Vigário Geral. The main Rio de Janeiro newspapers declared a truce and agreed to cooperate in a coordinated response. The sociologist and human rights activist Herbert de Souza, Brazil's 'conscience', known throughout the country as 'Betinho', was brought in to be the respected and trusted mascot of the movement. The movement's architect was Rubem César Fernandes, an academic closely linked to the Roman Catholic Church. It was a loose collection of public figures, intellectuals and activists. Initially, its agenda was symbolic. It aimed to mobilise Rio de Janeiro into large-scale public rejections of violence to create a commotion.

In this, it succeeded. Viva Rio hit a public nerve. It organised demonstrations calling for peace, held masses in remembrance of the dead. It even managed to bring most of Rio de Janeiro to a halt for two whole minutes of silence – an eternity of non-sound in Brazil's most voluble city. Eventually, Viva Rio would develop into a combination of think-tank and NGO. One person who was there from the beginning was Elisabeth Sussekind, a lawyer and academic. At the start of her career, during the dictatorship, she had worked for Fernando Fragoso, a lawyer famous for representing political prisoners.

'Some people said it was a demonstration of the rich. They made a lot of that point, that Viva Rio was a middle-class movement. The people in Viva Rio *were* middle class; they were people who had media careers, people who brought the Catholic Church with them. They brought in the main evangelical pastor of the time. What people said was that this whole movement was only happening because it was headed by those people, and they always asked members of Viva Rio, especially Rubem, if they were going to run for office. As if it were all in order to mobilise people so that they would vote for him later on. He never thought to run for office – he never wanted to. That was never in his plans, no way. But deep down, people who didn't know this mass social movement well believed that there had to be something behind it. As if the situation that they found themselves in, and about which they were demonstrating, was not enough. There had to be another reason for them to be doing that. It was always viewed with a lot of suspicion.

'Afterwards it became an NGO and the first eight years of Viva Rio were brilliant, because an NGO has a lot of flexibility of coverage. You have no bureaucracy. You don't have to ask permission. So Viva Rio was forceful in covering space that hadn't been covered before. But it also created jealousy. Rubem César had a lot of pull abroad. He was always very connected to the Catholic Church, and from the first moment he was able to get money. People thought that Viva Rio was swimming in money, but it wasn't. And people said that it was a piece of theatre. "Demonstrations on the beach – that's not going to solve anything!" "No. It won't solve anything. It's not meant to *solve* anything, it's meant to wake you up. To wake everyone up!" But people couldn't understand. Many of them still don't understand.'

Rio de Janeiro's NGO scene was notoriously and frustratingly incohesive. It fragmented in an undignified scramble for dwindling international funding, which, since the end of the 1980s, had started to move towards former Soviet Bloc countries. One of Viva Rio's harshest critics was Cristina Leonardo. She saw the movement as a lot of rich intellectuals doing nothing but talking and siphoning funds away from the grass roots, from the people who worked directly with the victims and their families. And she believed their concept of the 'Divided City' to be a strategic error. It was a phrase coined by the writer and Viva Rio activist Zuenir Ventura, and the title of his influential book. It talked for the first time of the two cities of Rio de Janeiro, the official and the unofficial, the paved and the unpaved. Cristina was unimpressed: 'The day that we divided the city, we created a great difficulty in joining and reuniting it: "You're *asfalto* – paving." "You're *favela*." It was a huge mistake at that time to accept that the city was divided.'

In time Cristina, who was never one to mince her words, would ensure that her dislike for Viva Rio was reciprocated. This mutual antipathy would have drastic consequences for Wagner's future.

11

Refuge in Bahia

THE FUSS OVER Vigário Geral had little impact on the day-to-day lives of the Candelária witnesses. They were moved to the witness house, attended identification parades and hearings. The Candelária files were riddled with statements reporting death threats. On their way back to the witness house late one night, Rogeirinho and Beth were stopped by off-duty police who threatened to kill them if they testified. On another occasion Marcelo had a call from Turinha, who was still on the streets. He was no longer at Candelária but had moved to Praça Mauá.

'Something had happened during the night,' said Marcelo. 'I went over there in the morning to find out what had happened. When I arrived there I met the boys. I don't remember any more what the story was – something about a car, someone going over to the group while they slept. I was talking to them with them facing me: Turinha, who's black, the other boy, who's also black. Suddenly their faces went white, looking over my shoulder. They said, "Look at that guy, *Tio*." When I looked there was a guy, and I remember him because he looked like my younger brother! And this guy threatened us like this: he stood in front of the boys at a finger's distance, face-to-face, and went from one to the other. He didn't say anything, and then he stood face-to-face with me. And then he left.'

The work at the *Centro Brasileiro* altered almost overnight. Many of the caseworkers did not want to go back onto the streets. Some thought it too dangerous. For others, like Marjorie, the massacre had thrown the nature of their work into doubt: 'I started to question the work that we were doing in the streets – whether we weren't legitimising the streets as a viable place for people to be.' The *Centro Brasileiro* went from carrying out hands-on individual case work with street children, to becoming a human rights defence centre, which represented victims of police violence. It was a different way of working and a different language. The Brazilian constitution, drawn up to consolidate the brand-new democracy, contained concepts of citizenship and human rights that were untested in a country that had lived with twenty-one years of military rule.

The caseworkers were slightly unsure of their new roles, and suspicious of the media attention that went with the *Centro Brasileiro's* new profile. 'I came to the conclusion that the media didn't help,' said Marcelo. 'My position was different from Cristina's. I don't know if it's because my mentality was very much that of a psychologist, who thinks in terms of preservation, of secrets. The press has a different way of protecting a person, which is super-exposure.' Marjorie was uncomfortable too: 'I think that the charities, including the *Centro Brasileiro*, became very involved with the media. The media was important, it helped to bring the case to trial, but my criticism is that the charities needed to behave appropriately towards the media, but they also needed to carry out grass roots work with the families. That was missing.'

Cristina, on the other hand, had found her vocation. She had always been concerned with citizenship, representation, encouraging people to understand their civil rights. The Candelária massacre had thrust her into a new role which allowed her to pursue this work from a different angle. Marcelo did not like the media, but he was impressed by the way in which Cristina embraced the challenge. 'Cristina carried out the legal role from the angle of a social movement. She was always pressuring the authorities. She forged alliances, organised, mobilised. I didn't see Cristina as *thinking* the legal role, but as *mobilising* the legal role. That she knew how to do well.'

Cristina was now representing the victims and their families in both Candelária and Vigário Geral, Brum was investigating both cases and Piñeiro and Assayag had 'won' the case lottery for Vigário Geral as well. Candelária had been the work of an 'immature' death squad, as Cristina put it, but the *Cavalos Corredores* were connected to a much larger, well-established network of corrupt police who specialised in extorting money from the *tráfico*. High-ranking police officers were implicated. Vigário Geral was a much more complex, dangerous and politically sensitive case. In Candelária, only the survivors and their carers received death threats; in Vigário, everyone up to and including the judge would experience them. Piñeiro and Assayag had also been assigned another extremely high-profile case: the murder of actress Daniela Perez, daughter of Brazilian soap scriptwriter Glória Perez, whose celebrity status ensured a media frenzy. Time and resources were stretched very thin and, inevitably, Candelária became the lower priority.

The lawyers and investigators barely had time to sleep. Yvonne's campaign – her vigil outside Candelária – was still going strong.

But to Wagner, idling away in the witness house, it felt as though the case had stagnated. He could not work. 'Who was going to give me work? No one wanted to employ me. Who would have the courage?' There was nothing to do at the witness house. His day consisted of taking food over the road and kicking a football around to get fit again after his long convalescence. He soon knew many of the residents, beggars and street vendors in the area. At night he went out looking for samba. Often he took a bus and went up to Mangueira to go to a *baile* – the huge dances that were organised in the *favela* football pitches, where the whole community turned out to drink and dance. During Carnaval he and his other friends from the witness house went to one of the massive samba halls and got into a fight. He was arrested, handcuffed, put into the police vehicle. The policemen, having realised that they had arrested the main witness in Candelária, did not really know what to do with him. They drove around and around, unlocked his handcuffs, and let him out back at the samba hall. 'More fighting! More samba!'

Eventually someone in authority tried to gain control of the situation. They replaced the police guard. They stopped the practice of giving away food. Someone came to upbraid the witnesses about their recklessness. 'After that I started to be angry,' said Wagner. 'I think that I was depressed.' He thought about this for a minute, trying to remember what he had been like back then, and then he laughed. 'I didn't know what depression was! But my life was passing me by. You start to feel hatred, rebelliousness.'

Cristina could see that she needed to get Wagner out of there. Thanks to a contact of American journalist John Maier, who had befriended Wagner while he was still in the hospital, she was able to secure Wagner a job in the north-east of the country, in a

Club Med resort in Bahia. In March 1994 she petitioned the judge for permission to move him. Wagner was only too glad to leave.

He was in Bahia for about eight months. He loved it there. Of all the states in Brazil, it was probably the most like Rio. It also looped along white beaches, and it also lived for music. Its capital, Salvador, never forgot that it was where the slave ships had docked, that it was the black soul of Brazil, and it referred back to Africa in every aspect of life: in the spicy, palm-oil based food, in the music, in the *capoeira* jousts on the steps of the colonial churches, in the fusion of African deities with Catholic saints. Wagner grew his hair and rolled it into dreadlocks. His colleagues nicknamed him Cariri, an affectionate take on *Carioca*. He worked at the hotel – landscaping, cleaning windows. He went to the beach.

Wagner was supposed to be in a secret location, but nothing stayed secret for long in Rio. A visiting journalist conducted a long interview with him for a Rio newspaper. Wagner was upbeat: 'Everything's back to normal.' Even the memory of the night of the massacre had faded: 'I only remember the bodies.' It was what he wanted: to forget. 'I want to have a normal life, a house, and later, children,' he said. Still, he was homesick. They did not have *bailes* in Salvador, and the poppy, reggae-based rhythms of Bahia were no substitute for his beloved samba. He felt no anger towards the people who had tried to kill him, he told the journalist. What he felt towards them was something hard to express, something more complex: 'What I feel for them is much more than anger.'[11]

It was too good to last. In November 1994 he was brought back to Rio to testify at a pre-trial hearing. When he arrived back in Salvador everyone had seen him on TV Globo's prime-time news. He was back to being the 'Candelária boy'. The sidelong glances started, the whisperings: '*marginal*, criminal, thief, street kid.' 'They started to harass me. And I tried to stay, I tried.' He told Cristina that he wanted to go back to Rio. She attempted to dissuade him, but he had made up his mind. He went to his employer in Salvador, thanked him for taking him on, apologised for leaving and flew home.

12

The Rio Comprido Link

WHILE WAGNER HAD been in Bahia the Candelária case had moved on. Brum had formed a very constructive working relationship with the prosecutors, Piñeiro and Assayag. It was unusual for a military policeman to be so closely involved with a civil police investigation, and more unusual still to be working in tandem with the prosecution service, but it made a lot of sense. Often there was a gap between the evidence turned up by a police investigation and the kind of evidence needed to make a case in court. In Candelária, the prosecutors involved themselves in the detail of the investigation in an unprecedented way. In time, Rio would formalise this model, and a police investigation unit would be attached to the Public Prosecution Service.

Cristina trusted Brum: 'He's an excellent investigator.' She persuaded him to take on other cases that she was representing. The victims and their families, who, being poor and usually black, were often forgotten and ignored, found that Brum had a sensitivity towards their trauma and grief that was rare in the police. He was often surly towards them. Cristina regularly ambushed him with victims, bereaved mothers and visiting international NGO delegates, and at times the clamour could cause him to lose his temper. But they saw him as an ally. Wagner spoke highly of him. It was Brum who had lent him the mandatory long trousers and long-sleeved shirt that he needed for his pre-trial court appearances.

The press loved Brum too. He was turning into something of a public hero. The media were intrusive and often inaccurate but, 'unfortunately, the media is the fuel which keeps the investigations going. Because if the media forgets about it, if it doesn't demand action, a lot of cases end up being archived. The media is very important, the healthy media, the investigative media, the media that holds the authorities accountable for the cases.' It was important to him on a personal level too. If he was being undermined by his own colleagues, he could rely on the media to support him: 'They know that my work is credible.'

Brum had been taking a closer look at the Candelária suspects. None of them had any history of criminal activity, but that only fitted with his sense that the massacre was spontaneous and ill thought out – shooting someone in the car had been a mistake, as had been leaving themselves with too many bodies to fit in the boots of their cars to dump elsewhere. He already believed that Cláudio, the black evangelical military policeman, had had nothing to do with the massacre. But when he started to look more closely at Emmanuel, his first impression – that Emmanuel was an unlikely candidate – started to change.

Emmanuel lived in the neighbourhood of Rio Comprido, and, while he might look as though butter would not melt in his mouth, it turned out that his brother had some very unsavoury friends. Chief among these was Maurício da Conceição Filho, a person so unpleasant that he had earned himself the nickname *Seixta-Feira 13* – Friday the 13th – and had even managed to get himself kicked out of the Military Police. Filho was one of Emmanuel's referees on his police application form.

Filho had been working as a security guard for a man known as Piruinha, who was running an illegal gambling network. Brum called him in for an interview. He was slight and black and looked a lot like Cláudio. But Brum never proceeded any further with Filho. Filho seemed to have had a falling out with his boss, who was now in jail, convicted for 'formation of a criminal band'. In March 1994, Filho and a few of his mates kidnapped Piruinha's grandson, tied him up, blindfolded him, demanded a ransom of US$100,000 and held him for three days before getting themselves shot dead by Civil Police who were acting on a tip-off. The grandson survived the ordeal, and according to a press report, 'met with friends, ate and had to take a tranquilizer in order to sleep.'

Brum was convinced that Filho was one of the men that the children had seen on the night of the massacre. He was now sure that the investigation had been looking in the wrong place. The crime did not centre on the Fifth Battalion, it centred on Rio Comprido. Then in May 1994 there was a breakthrough. A military policeman called Arlindo Lisboa Afonso Júnior was arrested for driving a stolen car. He was one of the Rio Comprido group of friends. Brum sent his gun off for ballistics testing. It turned out that it had been used in the massacre. Afonso denied any involvement in the massacre, and claimed that he had bought the gun from Filho. Brum did not believe him, but he could not disprove the story. Still, the prosecutors were able to charge him with obstruction of justice, and now Brum had the confirmation that he needed.

And then Brum was fired. A British TV crew, who presumably could not believe their luck, were there to film the moment.

Brum put the phone down: 'I've just been fired.' The phone rang again. 'Excuse me,' he said politely, and picked up the receiver. 'My friend,' he said. 'I've just been fired.' He put his hand over the receiver and asked the journalist, 'Do you mind if I swear?'[12]

It was nothing to do with Candelária or even Vigário Geral. He had been involved in another investigation which was getting a little too close to some people in high office. He had been accused of leaking information to the press. Officially, at least, he was off the Candelária case.

13

'O Corpo Fechado'
– 'A Closed Body'

WAGNER HAD BEEN back in Rio for about a week or two and was bored and restless in the witness house again. He had heard about a *baile* in one of the *favelas* and was determined to go. On the evening of 11 December 1995 he left the witness house to walk to the bus station at Rio's main station, *Central do Brasil*. It was dark already, and the city centre was emptying out. In front of *Central do Brasil* station the waiting commuter crowds milled about. The buses pulled up. The people surged on, clanking through the metal turnstiles one after the other. The buses moved off. The pavements refilled with people.

Wagner had just spotted his bus when a voice called out. Someone was asking him for a cigarette. He held out the pack, a cigarette protruding, then jumped on the bus. But it was the wrong one. He jumped off again.

Someone struck him on the shoulder. He stumbled a little and lost his bearings. It took him a couple of seconds to re-cover, and when he turned around he knew by instinct that the man who had hit him was a policeman. He started to run, dodg-ing through the crowds and in between the queuing buses. There was a bus coming, he was about to sprint across its path but a woman stood in his way, holding a baby. He stopped.

There were three men. One of them had his gun out. Another was pulling something out of his pocket, a newspaper clipping. It was a picture of Wagner. They handcuffed him to a fence in front of the station and all three of them started to beat him.

'Everyone saw,' said Wagner. 'Everyone knew who they were. A lot of people were stealing around there, they knew the police.'

Many of the people who worked at the station knew Wagner. A crowd had gathered. Wagner heard voices. 'Leave him alone!' 'What has he done?' 'Isn't that the Candelária boy?'

The men shouted back. 'We're police. He was robbing the bus! Look.' One of them put a hand in Wagner's pocket and made a pile of banknotes appear.

'Well, if he's done something, take him to the police station!' Among the faces, Wagner recognised someone – a boy with white patches on his skin. They had played football together at the orphanage. He called out his name, 'Domingos', just to anchor himself in the world. He thought it would help keep him safe to know someone. Domingos came over. He tried to tell the police that he knew Wagner, but one of them pushed a gun into his chest and told him it was none of his business. Domingos backed off, and disappeared into the crowd.

It was too much attention for the policemen. They released Wagner from the post and cuffed his hands behind his back. Wagner's arm was in plaster – he had sprained his wrist – and they struggled to close one of the cuffs. They started walking him along the front of the station, towards the entrance to the Metro. Commuters surged out of the huge Art Deco station, past the policemen and the bleeding Wagner, and down into the underground. Two of the policemen went down the steps to use the toilets, while one stayed with Wagner. 'What are you looking at?' he yelled. It was the universal language of thugs. Even at the time, it was impossible for Wagner not to laugh.

When the other two came back, Wagner could sense that the mood had changed, intensified. One of them – the black one with the scar under his moustache – was smiling. Wagner understood that his smile was dangerous, that 'things were about to heat up'. They walked him around the back of the bus station. Wagner could not see. His long fringe of dreadlocks was full of blood which kept dripping into his eyes. He stumbled as they pulled him along. He could just make out the feet of the people walking past. He heard one of the men demand water from a nearby vendor, and then felt the splash of water in his face. He could see again.

They dragged him through the bus station. 'Who sent you to Bahia, eh?' They were asking. 'Which judge was it?' They emerged on the other side of the bus station. There was a metal fence. It was quiet. The only people there were a couple of prostitutes. The men paid them no attention. They pushed Wagner against the fence and fired four bullets into him.

That was how he was found, slumped, unconscious and still wearing the handcuffs.

In the hospital the other patients joked that he had '*o corpo fechado* – a closed body'. If you lived in Rio, a body which was closed to attack by bullets, knives and poison was one of the things you were likely to petition the spirits for.

The press crowded into Wagner's hospital room. 'Would you recognise them again?' Wagner was sure that he would, but he was not sure he wanted to.

Just in case anyone wanted to use up any more of Wagner's several lives, one of the newspapers published the exact location of Wagner's bed: 'Bed 6 in the Ophthamology Department of Municipal Hospital Souza Aguiar.'

★

Cristina was furious with Wagner. 'Stubborn!' she said, which was quite something coming from her. 'I said to him, "Wagner, don't go out at night. Don't leave the house." "No. I've got a girlfriend" – it was something like that. I said to him, "If you keep going out like this I'm going to give up on you." There's even a document in the case files in which I suspend my representation of him. And that was on a Friday. On the Sunday my phone rings!'

The press released the story that Wagner had been robbing a bus. There was no investigation. Dozens of people, if not hundreds, had seen at least part of Wagner's arrest, beating and shooting but the case file consisted of little more than Wagner's statement and a couple of artist's impressions of the men involved. It seemed extraordinary, given the profile of the Candelária case, that the shooting of its star witness should simply disappear into an enormous pile of dejected blue cardboard files, and that no one had bothered to follow it up.

It was not Piñeiro's case, but even so the mention of it brought the slightest of ruffles to his otherwise smooth exterior. He shifted in his chair. 'As far as we were concerned he was in another state and then we heard there had been another attempt on his life. I'm convinced that it had nothing to do with the events at Candelária.' Even in Rio, it was disingenuous to suggest that a shooting, apparently by police, of a witness testifying against police, was likely to be purely coincidental, especially given that Wagner's attackers had known exactly who he was. But as far as Piñeiro was concerned, if there was no direct link with any of the defendants, which he did not believe – it was not in their interests, he said – then connecting it to Candelária could only confuse things for the prosecution. 'Everything suggests that what happened there was some kind of disturbance,' said Piñeiro, adding with the faintest tinge of frustration, 'It was something involving women.'

★

'I had a girlfriend in the witness house,' explained Wagner. 'And she asked to go with me, but I told her that I was going to a *baile* and that I'd pick her up afterwards. Only I was lying. After the *baile* I was planning to go to another girl's house.'

'What was your girlfriend's name?'

'Eliane. She was a witness in another case. I started going out with her when I got back from Bahia.'

'And you had another girlfriend somewhere else?'

'Valéria ... and Ana Paula.'

'*And* Ana Paula? You had three girlfriends?'

'Hey! Things were going well at the time!'

'You were ... what's the word in Portuguese? It's what you do with a ball.'

'Ping-pong?'

'No. More than one ball. You throw them in the air and catch them.'

'Juggling?'

'Yes. In English we would say that you were juggling women – because you can't hold more than one at the same time without things getting complicated.'

Wagner did not think that that was a very good metaphor. 'Yes you can,' he said. 'I was going out with two girls at the same time for a while. One slept on one side and the other on the other.'

★

Wagner's second shooting was treated as an embarrassing indiscretion that it was polite to ignore. Everyone had quite enough to deal with already, and Wagner was not helping by turning up half-dead in places he was not supposed to be. No suspects were ever questioned. No eye-witnesses interviewed. The case file disappeared for a few years, and when Brum asked for it to be dug out again in 2005, it turned out that Wagner had never even undergone the *corpo de delito* – the forensic medical examination required to formally register a crime.

Wagner could not pretend that it had never happened, however. The second shooting was far more severe in its consequences that the first, not only psychologically, but physically. He had been shot four times. A bullet had passed through his shoulder. Two others, which damaged his lungs, were removed. The bullet to his head had shattered on the vertebrae at the back of his neck, causing total paralysis to the right side of his face. His eye, cheek and mouth drooped. His eyesight and his hearing were permanently damaged. He was severely disfigured, and, with the disfigurement, even more easily recognisable than he had been before.

PART III

Testimony

14

Secret Investigations

THE PUBLIC PROSECUTORS had a dilemma. They were now convinced that one of the defendants, Emmanuel, was guilty. They were also convinced that Cláudio was innocent. They were not so sure about Cortes and Jurandir, but they had to consider the possibility that they too were innocent; so far they had found nothing to link them to Emmanuel. Brum's investigation had led them to the Rio Comprido group, and they now had some hope that they would be able to make further arrests. They were still working on the principle that two cars and up to eight men had been involved.

It was a delicate ethical question. The only solid evidence they had were the eyewitness identifications. If they admitted that any of those identifications were unreliable then the defence would ensure that all four defendants would walk free, and no one would ever stand trial for the Candelária massacre. If they kept quiet, they were keeping an innocent man in jail for a number of years – possibly three innocent men.

Technically, they were not hiding anything from the defence. In Brazil, the Civil Police inquiry is separate from legal proceedings. If the *Delegado* believes that there is a case against a suspect he makes a report to the Public Prosecution Service.

Then, in the case of homicide, which is triable by jury, there is a two-phase process. In the first investigative phase, all the evidence, including statements by witnesses, is heard and documented in written form before a judge in the presence of prosecution and defence lawyers – this phase is fully adversary. The judge then rules whether or not there is sufficient evidence to move to the second phase: a jury trial. So, in the Candelária case, as long as the new evidence about the Rio Comprido group remained within the Civil Police investigation, it did not have to be disclosed to the defence.

Piñeiro and Filho struggled with their consciences. 'So many nights we asked ourselves, "What are we going to do?" It wasn't easy. We could have asked for them to be freed. But just as we didn't ask, there came a time when their defence lawyers stopped asking. And I have no doubt that they realised that something was going on in the case, that the prosecutors were pursuing a new line. They must have believed that we were getting there.'

The eventual outcome, he felt, had vindicated them. But back in 1994 the outcome was not at all assured. The only defendant of whose guilt they were certain did not look like any jury's idea of a killer. He was quite likely to be acquitted. 'He had an alibi from his mother and friends who said that he had been at home at that time. The papers displayed their prejudiced side: Emmanuel is white, good-looking, even, of French origins. There were people who said that someone like that would never take part, that is to say, because he was white he couldn't have participated, only a black man would have done so. So there was that type of prejudice. We had that to face. In addition, my society – Rio de Janeiro, São Paulo, the big centres – suffers from a lot of violence. There are a lot of muggings, thefts, killings which are carried out by boys who are on the streets. There's a social revulsion. Many people sent letters to the papers saying that it was not the Candelária *chacina* – massacre – it was the Candelária *faxina* – spring clean. We had to confront this barrier of discrimination. It was very hard for me, my colleagues, Cristina, Yvonne. We had to overcome this barrier.'

There was no real choice to make. The prosecutors had to bring the case to trial. On the one hand, their discomfort at keeping potentially innocent men in jail for a year or two longer was far outweighed by their moral repugnance at the idea of letting all the perpetrators go free. On the other, the implications of allowing Candelária to fall apart would be disastrous for their personal and professional reputations. The case was a national and international *cause célèbre*. It had been reported all over the world, foreign television crews came to Rio to record documentaries about the massacre, letters from Amnesty International volunteers petitioning the Rio and Federal authorities to protect the witnesses and bring the killers to justice were arriving by the sackful.

Since November 1994, Brazil had a new president, Fernando Henrique Cardoso, a former political exile with a stated commitment to human rights protection. One of his first steps in office was to create a Secretariat for Human Rights within the Ministry of Justice, and he had placed his old friend and former civil rights lawyer, José Gregori, in the post. The new administration wished to dignify Brazil's international reputation, especially after the spectacularly soap-operatic collapse of the Collor government. The Candelária show had to go on.

Brum was officially off the case, but unofficially he carried on working with the prosecutors. Piñeiro and Assayag found themselves in the incongruous position of conducting a secret investigation in order to prove the innocence of three of the people that they were being paid to prosecute. It was unorthodox, to say the least. And as for their star witness, Wagner: by the time he suffered the second attempt on his life, the one that would destroy his health and self-esteem forever, the prosecutors had come to the conclusion that at least one of his identifications was unsound.

15

Second Time Around

WAGNER WAS BACK in a barren hospital room with police guards at his door. After his first shooting he had been bewildered and bored, but fired with a sense of justice and buoyed up by a belief that he had been saved for a purpose. Now, he felt vulnerable and alone. When he looked in the mirror he did not recognise his face; he appeared to himself as something that was frightening to children. He had almost no visitors. His friends had all disappeared. He did not blame them: 'They were afraid. Not now – nowadays I meet with them, they come to see me.' It was hard, all the same. But one woman did come to see him, to sit by his bedside and cry for her lost son who had been beaten to death on a bus by a security guard.

The hospital wanted Wagner out. A couple of weeks after the shooting they received an anonymous phone call from someone threatening to abduct him from his bed. They immediately tried to discharge him. He was moved to the Fire Service Hospital, and within a couple of days it too received a telephone call, threatening an invasion of the hospital. The hospital prepared to defend itself. In retrospect it seemed funny to Wagner, who lay in his bed while some thirty agitated men armed with machine guns ran around him, as if on fast forward. He laughed: 'Anyone with heart problems would have died that day!'

There was no invasion of the hospital, but on his night shifts, one of the guards would come in and shake his bed and tell him that he was going to kill him. It went on for weeks. 'They tortured me. Psychologically disturbed me. The only reason they didn't kill me was because I was so disturbed that I didn't sleep.' Wagner stopped taking his medication; he thought they might kill him that way. 'I put it in my mouth and then went to the bathroom and spat it out.'

Many of the threats involved his identification of Cortes: that he would be killed if he did not withdraw it, if he did not testify that it was Cortes who had helped him. He kept quiet about it, but Cristina was keeping an eye on him. 'When I went to visit Wagner I found him very sad, very strange, very upset. He wasn't making sense. He said that he didn't want me to go there any more. I thought, "Something's going on with Wagner." I left my phone number with a nurse and said, "If there's any strange activity, call me." Then one day in the afternoon – I was at home, all untidy, in total confusion, I'd just come back from the beach – the nurse called my mobile phone: "Dona Cristina come quickly!" I was lucky that my house is in Tijuca and the hospital is in Rio Comprido. And she was saying, "Cortes's lawyer is here putting pressure on Wagner." I left the house dressed as I was, in rubber sandals, and when I got to the hospital Cortes's lawyer was putting pressure on Wagner to change his testimony, with everything prepared, all he needed to do was sign. When I got there I said, "Well this is nice!" I took the lawyer outside. That's when another patient told me that at night they went into

Wagner's room and wouldn't give him any peace and quiet to sleep.'

Cristina recorded Wagner's complaints and passed them on to the prosecutors who in turn passed them on to the judge. The judge asked the state to find a more secure hospital arrangement. The state suggested that federal military hospitals might be the answer. The Federal Government failed to respond to the suggestion.

One of the policemen who had threatened him eventually turned up on the television in Minas Gerais state, where he was being arrested for kidnapping the daughter of the state governor. Later, another of his guards would be investigated for accepting bribes. He had to laugh not to cry: 'I said to myself, "These are the kind of people who are looking after me!"'

Wagner wrote to Cristina. The effort that writing cost him was evident in his painstaking capital letters and his spelling mistakes. He addressed her as *Tia*, which was oddly childlike coming from a grown man, but it was what the Candelária kids had called her, and it was apt in the context of their relationship. She was an authority figure, like an aunt or teacher; her influence on him was profound. He feared letting her down.

Rio 3 April 1995

Tia Cristina,

I'd like to ask you if you could arrange somewhere for me to stay until my trial, because I can't stay here in hospital. They have put me in a room where I'm not allowed to walk in the corridor or talk to people, leaving me incommunicado. I know that this is not necessary. I understand that they are treating me like a prisoner. Even prisoners have a right to take the sun and talk to people that they feel comfortable with. Why take this away from me if I'm not a prisoner?

Even worse, if when the trial is over the accused are not convicted they will have the same liberty that I still have to win, and I will have been detained for the same amount of time, for having done nothing. If it's possible, arrange a place where I have security and liberty, somewhere where I feel comfortable. I'd like this to be recognised, because I've already spent half of my life detained is some form in the orphanages where I was interned. I know that I've had a lot of suffering in my life, but I know that it was a quirk of fate. I couldn't change what was written. I could just avoid it happening, but as it has happened it's no one's fault. I have known suffering since I was six years old. There's no mystery to suffering for me. But I never thought that I would have to go through what I've been going through for the last two years. I was able to overcome my other suffering because I had friends and colleagues, but I can't take any more of being imprisoned without these friends and colleagues for something I haven't done.

Wagner

Wagner's resolve was wearing thin. Cristina realised that they were on the verge of losing his cooperation. The issue of his safety had become a crisis. Cristina was not just working her telephone and banging on doors in Brazil. In London, daily faxes arrived at the Amnesty International offices with Cristina's enormous dramatic diagonal scrawl covering four pages, when just one would have sufficed. She exploited the *Carioca* and federal sensitivity about Brazil's international image, and regularly threatened the authorities with 'Amnesty International' in the press, as if it had magical powers. It did not have magical powers, but in April 1995 it did have the full attention of the Brazilian media. Its Secretary-General, Pierre Sané, was on a visit to Brazil to meet with new President, Fernando Henrique Cardoso. It was a revelation to melting-pot Brazil, to discover that the man at the head of the world's largest human rights organisation was a black African. The press followed him everywhere. He toured the *favelas*, warmly shook hands with Vigário Geral survivors and mothers of disappeared teenagers and he took the Rio press right to Wagner's bedside.

'That was when everything changed,' said Wagner. Suddenly, everyone remembered that he existed. A couple of weeks after Pierre Sané's visit, Wagner was referred to another hospital and a judge ordered that he should receive plastic surgery to attempt to rescue his destroyed face. Brazil boasted some of the best plastic surgeons in the world, and the surgeon, Thomas Nassif, was optimistic. The bullet had lodged at the back of the neck, damaging the facial nerve, but he believed that he could wire up Wagner's face again so that the right side would work in tandem with the left: 'We take nerve grafts and lengthen the nerves from the good side to the paralysed side. The great advantage of this operation is that you get synchronicity of movement. The trigger for the movement comes from the same place: I close an eye, the other closes; I smile with one side of the mouth and the other smiles.

'This surgery is done in two phases. In the first we connect the nerves. These are fine nerves that we take from the leg. We connect the good side and pass them over to the other side and leave them loose. Then we wait six months, which is the time it takes for the nerve to grow. Six months later we operate on the paralysed side and connect the nerves to the musculature. But if the second operation isn't done, nothing happens.'

The first operation went well, but Wagner never received the second operation. The Pierre Sané effect was short-lived. It would be eight years before Thomas Nassif would see his patient again. By that time it would be too late, the muscles had atrophied. 'Our first operation was thrown in the bin,' said Nassif. 'It was useless, lost.'

★

Wagner could not stay in hospital forever. There was nowhere to go but back to the witness house. He was desperately unhappy. Cristina turned to Andrea.

Andrea had been battling with her own demons since Candelária. Once the roller-coaster experience of seeing the survivors through the aftermath of the massacre was over, she found herself in a deep depression. 'I was in a catatonic state for months,' she said, casually, as if describing a head cold. 'I was obsessed by who gave the order for the massacre.' She was still fragile, but was now back at work, and Cristina assigned her to work with Wagner as his therapist.

They had barely met. They had seen each other from a distance at the party on the night before the massacre, and at the various identifications and hearings when Andrea was accompanying other witnesses. Andrea was horrified by the witness house. 'No one deserves to stay in a place like that. It was dreadful.' Her first impression of Wagner was of how well he was able to get on with others. He was clearly very troubled, but still he 'had a good relationship with the police. He was a generous person. He got on well with his guards.'

There is a word in Portuguese: *carinho*. It baldly translates into English as 'affection', but it's a quality of human contact that belongs to hot climates. It's in the tone of voice when people talk to children; it's in the touch of a hand on an arm during a conversation. Andrea had *carinho* in abundance – she was passionate about people. Wagner had had little enough *carinho* in the last couple of years. He took to Andrea immediately. It would become a great friendship, the first that Wagner could rely on since he had left the orphanage.

Andrea was small and graceful – the other passion in her life was dance – and barely came up to Wagner's collarbone. They both loved music and the Botafogo football team and joking around with people. But their light-heartedness masked a deeper seriousness, and when they settled down to talk, the full extent of the damage done to Wagner soon became clear.

Andrea was a comfort to Wagner, but she could not do anything about what he identified as the main cause of his unhappiness, which was that he effectively remained a prisoner. And while Cristina was doing everything she could to persuade Wagner to stay involved, Andrea's responsibility towards him, as his therapist, placed obligations upon her which were at odds with Cristina's priorities as a lawyer: 'Cristina was always telling him what he had to say. And, as I was there as a psychologist, I tried to show him what he wanted to say. So on various occasions

I raised the subject of the conflict that he was experiencing between the things that Cristina asked him to do and the things that *he* wanted. And the moment arrived when he said that he didn't want to be part of the case any more. I clarified to him what not taking part signified, that he would have to go to the judge and sign and stop being a witness and that by stopping being a witness he would no longer have protection. At the same time the crazy thing was that he wanted to see a resolution. This is a characterisic which is very strong in Brazilian culture of wanting to bring out the truth – we experience this very forcefully here, especially humble people. And I told him that if he left the witness protection the case would die. It was him who was keeping the case going! Who else was there?'

Wagner went to court and asked to be relieved of any further court appearances. He still remained a state witness, and committed to keeping in contact with the court and to considering further appearances at a later stage, provided that he received protection. Technically, his identifications and statements had already been secured and his withdrawal did not affect jury trial stage, but in practice his withdrawal presented problems for the ongoing investigation and for the jury trial itself, during which the prosecutors were relying on the dramatic flourish of Wagner's presence. In a letter which he presented to the court he addressed the hundreds of Amnesty International volunteers who had sent him letters of support and encouragement.

> *I thank all those in Amnesty International for everything that they have done for me but I can no longer endure continuing what I started. Over time, I have exhausted myself too much. I have many reasons; I spent a long*

time fighting against the system in my Brazil. At the
beginning, many people warned me and I didn't want to
believe them. Today I see that it's the truth. I'm drained
by everything that has happened. I fought as long as I
could, but I can't any more. Forgive me my weakness,
because you wrote to me. I know that you have an idea of
what I'm like, but I can't take any more. At the moment
I just want to think about my future, forget the past, find
work, build a small home; things that I've never had –
just living in an institution, living at work ... if I hadn't
lived like that this would never have happened to me
because at that time I would have been under my own
roof but unfortunately I was there because I had nowhere
to live.

It has been difficult to take this decision, but I believe
that it's time, because Brazilian justice leads nowhere.
So they have defeated me with tiredness. I thank you all.
Thank you very much for everything that you've done
for me to try to give me strength and courage. I'll finish
here. I'm finishing. I'm sorry to all who have supported
me and believed my story. One day, when there is a more
dignified and humane country and a fair fight ... I don't
feel defeated, but I do feel exhausted by the length of the
battle. I can say battle, because of the suffering it has
caused to me and to those who have helped me.

Cristina persisted in her campaign for the state to find alternative
safe accommodation for him, always hopeful that if they could
resolve that issue, Wagner might return to the case. At the end
of September 1995 the public prosecutors suggested that he be

moved to a Military Police barracks in Niteroi. It was where fourteen of the military police accused of participation in the Vigário Geral massacre were being held. It did not sound particularly safe to Wagner. He was out of resources. He tried to kill himself.

The suicide attempt was the one thing that Wagner could not talk about. The rest was painful, but that dark moment in his life when he cut his wrists was impossible to discuss.

16

Running and Hiding

YVONNE EXPRESSED TO the media a fury that Wagner was too weary to feel for himself. It had been conditions inside the witness house that had led him to attempt suicide, she told them. Wagner had told her that he had 'been defeated by the system'. She elaborated on his behalf: 'It makes no sense that a person who's not a defendant in anything, who is simply a witness to a crime, should have to live as if he were in a prison. Two years after the massacre the case still hasn't come to court!' He would not, she insisted, be testifying: 'He's already told everything he knows and everything he saw. He has nothing more to say.'[13]

Cristina characterised the event not as an attempted suicide but as an attempted murder: 'They did everything they could to kill Wagner. Everything. So much so that he tried to cut his wrists. They'd noticed that Wagner was fragile, so they started to brainwash him. At night they wouldn't let him sleep: they made a lot of noise, they threatened him. And Wagner was already debilitated ...'

The *Centro Brasileiro* had come to the conclusion that Wagner would be better off under their protection than that of the state. Cristina went to fetch him out of the witness house. 'I entered the witness house with the police on my back. I said, "It won't do you any good to restrain me." I put my foot in the door and said, "Wagner, the only thing you're taking from here is the television!" Then Wagner behind me, me pulling Wagner, the police behind me: "You can't do this!" and I said, "I am doing this."'

Cristina secured judicial authorisation to assume responsibility for Wagner's safety. One of her contacts in Rio's human rights community was able to offer Wagner her grandmother's country house. Another contact offered to drive him there, in the company of Andrea. 'When we arrived at this town we stopped to drink water and someone recognised Wagner! Amazing! It was amazing how destructive the amount of exposure of his image was. It's a face that no one in Brazil has forgotten! That's why he's always at risk. And this worried us. It became clear to us that he could only stay in a place for fifteen to twenty days at a time until we could find somewhere permanent for him to stay.'

In retrospect, this period of his life elongated into months of experience, but in fact it was only a matter of a few fraught weeks, and no one could be certain of the exact order of events. Andrea accompanied Wagner on each of his moves, 'Always terrified that we might be being followed.' A couple of weeks after his move to the interior, Cristina found him a place in a drug rehabilitation centre. Wagner found it utterly humiliating. He had to undergo a strip search to enter the institution, and was then surrounded by drug addicts, which did little to restore his equilibrium. He phoned Andrea daily to complain that it was unbearable.

Cristina talked one of her friends into lending her a beach house in Itaipuaçu. The plan was flawed, because her friend's husband could not know that Wagner was hidden there. 'And then my friend's husband decided to have a barbecue, and Wagner remained hidden while he was doing the barbecue,' Cristina remembered. 'My friend felt desperately sorry for Wagner, because she had to lock him in a room, so she decided to take him for a walk on the beach to give him some coconut water. Only she talked to me a lot on the phone and they tracked her cellphone! The police almost killed him and my friend! They were walking along the beach, the police car stopped, they surrounded them. They took Wagner and Wagner told them to let my friend go. He said he was Wagner of Candelária and went with them. My friend managed to call me on my cellphone. TV Globo went to Itaipuaçu by helicopter. It was TV Globo who saved him.'

Cristina was the legal profession's equivalent of a fist-fighter. Marjorie had said that she belonged in a detective novel. She loved a good brawl, was apparently fearless, and animatedly re-counted her battle yarns with a liberal peppering of exclamation marks. 'My friend was in hospital for a month with depression and a nervous breakdown,' said Cristina, with a chordal laugh. 'It was mayhem!'

Wagner's recollection of this incident was slightly different to Cristina's. In his version they were at the beach *because* Cristina had pre-arranged an interview with TV Globo, but he was used to Cristina's embellishments, and shrugged his shoulders in resignation, as he so often did.

Andrea was furious. As ever, she was deeply suspicious of Cristina's relationship with the media: she perceived it as a Faustian pact that must eventually exact the price of a soul, probably Wagner's. The episode, she said, understating what had been her reaction at the time, had been 'lamentable'. But whether or not it had been an irresponsible act or a stroke of campaigning genius on Cristina's part, one thing was becoming clear: they could not hope to keep Wagner safe in the state of Rio de Janeiro.

17

Back on the Case

BRUM HAD BEEN suspended from duty, but, on- or off-duty, he was permanently immersed in the swirl of noxious mist that was Military Police battalion gossip and intrigue. There was no secrecy in the force, only a code of silence, and every so often a betrayal of confidence might be bartered for.

'I returned to active duty in 1995,' said Brum. 'I took command of a battalion and used the structure of that battalion to continue investigating the Candelária massacre. I had never lost contact with the prosecutors. I was reviled in the police force, but I'd never lost credibility with the prosecutors.'

Brum was always out of place, somehow. Around him people ate lunch, packed tightly around square tables decked with white tablecloths. The waiters, stocky men with southern European features in white jackets, squeezed between tables. Plates of grilled meat, rice and fried potatoes sailed over the heads of their customers, who were also white and solidly middle-class. The men wore their black hair cropped; the long hair of the few women was chemically highlighted a couple of shades lighter. They wore clothing that had survived an entire morning of Rio's heat and humidity thanks to the skilled washing, ironing and starching of their dark-skinned maids. Looking at Brum, there was little to distinguish him from his fellow diners – he was a little thinner, perhaps; a little more careworn. Demographically speaking, this was where he belonged. This was where he chose to eat lunch. Yet he knew that these were also the people who had applauded the deaths of the Candelária kids. He led a lonely life.

'So,' he said, ladling stroganoff onto his rice, 'I was investigating for the Public Ministry – an informal relationship. I was in command of the Shock Battalion and I discovered a few things because the battalion had a prison. One of the prisoners, who was obviously looking for some kind of deal and who knew that I was investigating Candelária, gave me some information about the massacre. He had been involved in another homicide, and he confirmed everything that I already believed. I was already almost certain that the connection was geographical – that is to say, that they were friends from the same neighbourhood. And he gave us the names and we went about confirming them.'

'One day,' said Piñeiro, 'Brum calls us. We go to the battalion, in Rua Africaneca, in front of the prison complex. He says, "A prisoner has given me information about the group." And we listened to him, in front of Brum, in his cell, and this prisoner gave us information, confirming the existence of the group. He didn't receive anything in exchange for these confessions. He hadn't participated in the massacre, but he gave details that confirmed our understanding. Apart from that, in Vigário Geral they were practically all Military Police who were being detained in a Shock Battalion, and in the Shock Battalion there were other police prisoners, and two policemen, who were Vigário Geral defendants, talked to Brum and then we took them to the Civil Police. They had learnt things in prison and had heard names;

one of them was 'Cunha', who was a man of whom we already knew. You can imagine: in prison, all Military Police who are detained for various reasons, one for Candelária, the other for Vigário, for this, for that ... And they're talking, "*Po!* You were involved in that?" "Yes." And so on. What happened? Two Vigário defendants gave formal statements. In the prison we heard various names, names which coincided with those we were investigating. We went to the police station, we took them there to formalise everything, they gave statements, made allegations, and named names.'

One of the names was Marco Aurélio Dias Alcântara. Alcântara's name had already come up in Emmanuel's profile. Like Filho, he had been a referee on Emmanuel's application to join the Military Police. Brum had a theory about Alcântara, and he invited Piñeiro to join him in a little bit of espionage at the battalion, 'as if we were having a coffee together to talk about Public Ministry business, but really, knowing that Alcântara went there. We took a look at him without him noticing anything: "That's Alcântara there." "Damn!" – the chip in the tooth – "He looks exactly like Cortes!"'

Brum's theory was this: Cortes *had* attended to Wagner at the petrol station, but that he had not been in the car with the shooters, and that it was Alcântara, who looked like Cortes, who had been there. In Wagner's traumatised mind, they now believed, the faces had been exchanged. He was telling the truth, but he was reporting a false memory. There was no connection at all between the massacre and the Fifth Battalion.

This presented them with a number of strategic problems: how were they to turn their hunch into evidence that might be presented in court without upsetting Wagner, without alerting

Cristina to their subterfuge and without tipping off the suspects that they were under investigation? And how were they to secure what they needed from Wagner, given that he was not prepared to make any more pre-trial court appearances? 'In truth,' said Piñeiro, 'we had to come up with a scheme, because there was no reason for him to appear at any more hearings – only at the trial.'

Wagner was asked if he would be prepared to attend another pre-trial hearing. 'I said no, I wouldn't, because it was impossible. In almost everything I was doing, I had no support – I had no support, I had nothing that might help me. And that was when the President said that it would be better if I went to Brasília if I would agree to go back to being a witness.'

For some time, Amnesty International had been lobbying the Brazilian Federal Government to take responsibility for Wagner's security. Under the new constitution, it fell upon the Federal Government to ensure adherence to human rights protection legislation within the states, and to intervene where states failed to comply. Rio had clearly failed to provide security for Wagner. Finally, in October 1995, the Federal Government stepped in and offered Wagner protection. Cristina told Wagner that the invitation to Brasília had been made by President Cardoso himself. It was the sort of request that is hard to refuse, and, in any case, he could not sustain the nomadic existence he was leading in Rio state. Wagner accepted the proposal.

'We arranged for him to come from Brasília to make a statement in our parallel investigation, but using the Candelária proceedings to seek a link between the two murder attempts,' said Piñeiro. 'In principle the second attempt had nothing to do with the massacre, but we used it as a ploy. I admit that it was a ploy. It was a way of justifying his presence.' In court they showed Wagner a number of photos, ostensibly to examine the possibility of a connection with the second attempt on Wagner's life. One of the photos was that of Alcântara. 'We set out a photo. It was amplified and very clear. Cristina Leonardo was present. He looked at the new person, Marcos Aurélio Dias Alcântara: "I recognise him." That was all I wanted. He recognised Alcântara as a person that he had seen on the day, but he didn't go into details. It wasn't in our interests to ask any more at that stage, because the defence lawyers would have noticed. It was a tactic. We couldn't invalidate a proof. We had to guarantee it. The judge knew all about it.'

Wagner gave a statement to the media on the steps of the court and was then led off by his federal guards. As far as the journalists were concerned he was being taken to the airport to return to Brasília. In fact, Brum had just taken him around to the back of the court and into Piñeiro's office where Piñeiro asked him: '"How do you know this man? What do you remember?" There was no press or judge. It was just us, without the defence lawyers, and he said, "That's the one who helped me at the petrol station." That was Wagner's statement. He saw Alcântara's photo: "This is who helped me." I said, "Wagner, try hard to remember. You said that the person in the car was Marcelo Cortes, and you are staying that this is the person you mentioned in your statement, who talked to you and told you to not to turn your face." "This is him. This is the one who helped me." He didn't know, and we didn't let him know, because he might have been offended. Because I think that he was worried – and I talked about this with Cristina – that he might be discredited. And he was the main witness!'

18

The Move to Geneva

In October 1995, Wagner was living at the Federal Police Academy in Brasília and had found a job with a mechanic, washing cars and buses. He was glad to be somewhat independent again. But Brasília, a futuristic fantasy of a city, built almost as far away from the sea as was possible, held little charm for him. It was not a city in which he could take off and walk, as he liked to – it had been designed for cars, not pedestrians. And the dry, red-dusty heat seemed harsh compared to the maritime humidity of his home. He was beginning to discover that there was no place for him but the one place that he could not be.

He had been in Brasília for about a month when a policeman came in and told him to put on his shirt because he had a visitor. Unconsciously, the words 'put your shirt on, you have a visitor' brought to mind prison guards instructing prisoners to make themselves respectable because a priest or lawyer or visiting dignitary was on the wing. It was a reminder that, wherever he was in Brazil, his protectors demanded a deference and compliance from him that they would never have expected had he been middle-class and white. Wagner did not like politics, and, when asked how he would describe his skin colour, did not say '*negro*' as a politically-conscious black Brazilian would do. Instead, he sidestepped with a jokey and percussive, *'marrom bom-bom'* – chestnut candy. It was a good, if dismissive, answer. It revealed as much as he wished to about himself: he would not be drawn on the race question, that he had a good sense of rhythm, and that his skin was exactly the colour of chestnut candy. Even so, he was well aware that his skin colour influenced the way that he was treated and the decisions that were made on his behalf.

The visitor was Dr José Gregori, Federal Secretary for Human Rights, and personal friend of the President. According to Wagner 'it was all very quick. He introduced himself, said, "I'm the Secretary for Human Rights here in Brasília and I've come to tell you that you're going to Switzerland for three months to train to work in a hotel,"' Wagner remembered. 'I was surprised. But I wanted to go because it was something new. I had the opportunity to lead a different life. I didn't want to get old and die where I was.'

Wagner thought he was going for three months. Eleven years later he was still there. He had never known how and why the decision was taken to send him to Switzerland, but it was not hard to find out. Gregori had turned to Viva Rio to solve the Wagner problem, as Elisabeth Sussekind explained. Viva Rio had recently set up a witness protection project and Elisabeth had put together a proposal and presented it to Gregori for funding. Gregori had put Viva Rio in touch with a northeastern NGO called GAJOP, which, for some time, had been developing its own witness protection programme in the state of Pernambuco. Constructing a witness protection programme which had to function independently of the police was quite a challenge, and it was groundbreaking work. Viva Rio looked at what GAJOP were doing, and with their help set about adapting the programme to fit the demands of the state of Rio de Janeiro. Eventually, GAJOP's project would become the blueprint for a national witness protection programme.

'And then one day, Dr Gregori phoned Rubem late in the afternoon, very discreetly, and said, "I need you to hide a witness for me." Rubem said, "Fine. We'll look into it." No one said who it was. Gregori didn't tell Rubem. Rubem didn't tell me. After a while, I started to want more information about the person. At least we needed to know his age; we needed to know what he did in order to see where we could place him. Sometimes we hid people in our homes. We needed to know the level of danger – what threat there was to the person, and what threat to whomever was looking after him. Eventually we found out who it was. I thought, *Caramba*! This is going to be really difficult! It will have to be outside Rio.'

A typical case for Viva Rio was someone who was trying to leave the *tráfico*. The fledgling programme had never had to deal with a high-profile witness like Wagner. In fact, there had never been a high-profile witness like Wagner before. Elisabeth, like everyone else involved with Wagner's security so far, had to improvise.

Viva Rio had a volunteer working for them who divided her life between Rio and Geneva, and who ran a charity called *Comité Pour La Vie* – Committee for Life. Maria Bourgeois was a former model, and her husband had been Swiss. She had set up a small project in Vigário Geral in the form of a beauty salon, training girls in hairdressing and beauty therapy. She also ran a little restaurant in the city which she staffed with trainees recruited from *favelas*. It was a modest and maternalistic approach, dismissed by her critics as being old-fashioned. But Maria was not interested in social politics. Her husband had died when he was only fifty, and the loss had floored her. 'He had cancer, and I suddenly realised that life wasn't what I'd thought – living in luxury. I'd been a model, travelled the whole world, I thought myself wonderful, but one day reality hit me and I saw that that's not what life's about. I had children – they were wonderful – but suddenly I had this shock. I was in such pain. I was in love – I still am ... When I heard about my husband's cancer I made a promise. I wanted to see my children grow up. I promised that if God would leave me my children I would save people. And he left them to me and so I have this obligation.'

In Geneva, Maria was helping Viva Rio to raise funds for a crèche for Vigário Geral, and Elisabeth was planning to travel there to make a presentation. Elisabeth talked to Rubem César: '"Why don't we try to take him there, abroad, at least for a while until things blow over. No one will be able to find him" – because he really was being hunted. Then we asked Maria to find somewhere where he could be housed. I didn't want him to stay in her house, because she had three sons. And she used her contacts among her friends and found an ideal situation for Wagner. He would be in a restaurant. We went to visit the restaurant and talked to the guy. And it was a sort of concession. They didn't want to do it officially through the Brazilian government because then people would know where he was. It was all informal, without being illegal. It was ...' Elisabeth searched for the right expression, and, waving her hand in the air, came up with the two words that least described Switzerland, '... slightly irregular.'

Wagner had no possessions to pack. The Ministry of Justice had magicked up a passport for him. A federal agent saw him onto the plane. He was met in transit in Zurich by someone from the Brazilian Consulate who bought him a coffee and saw him to the plane to Geneva. It was November, but no one had taken the northern European winter into account. It was snowing in Geneva, and Wagner was wearing a training suit and rubber sandals.

Elisabeth and Maria met him in Geneva. 'He was a little lost,' said Elisabeth, 'but lucid, normal. He liked the idea. He was happy to be there. But he was in a bad way, a really bad way.' He was not at all what they had expected. 'He was a lot bigger than I'd thought; I had been imagining someone a lot smaller. Which was problematic: a black boy, a boy who didn't have any skills, and with problems. He was a boy who had known violence, who had experienced extreme want. It affects people. I didn't know what his life would be like there.'

For her part, Maria was shocked by his disfigurement. It was as if the outward damage suddenly led her to understand that this was not going to be as straightforward as it had seemed in theory. Certainly they were both frightened. 'It had been very dangerous for us,' said Elisabeth. 'For me, personally, it was very dangerous doing all of this. When I went home I was very anxious, because I had small children and all of that.' Maria had insisted that Wagner come on Swissair – not trusting the discretion of a Brazilian airline. 'When he arrived I was frightened about what might happen to him, because people might come after him. Those people have money – those people who kill, they have connections as well.'

They were probably also frightened, at least initially, by Wagner himself, by what he represented. They knew nothing about him, only what had been consistently misreported in the press: he had been a street child. They did not know, for example, that he had worked and that he had experience as a baker. The person who could have provided them with an accurate profile of Wagner was Andrea, but, as Cristina and Viva Rio would have nothing to do with each other, she was never asked.

Also at the airport was a contact of Maria's, a colonel in the Swiss army, Monsieur Barraud. He had fixed things with his contacts to enable Wagner to enter the country, and had accompanied Wagner through immigration and customs. Just in case of prying eyes, Barraud took Wagner down to the train station and away from Geneva, to sneak him back some time later. Barraud had arranged for Wagner to work and live in his restaurant, which was in the central train station. Maria characterised what he was doing as a *'stage'* in the kitchen – gaining work experience, with full board and lodging, and earning 500 Swiss francs (£200/US$400) a month. Wagner was not the only Brazilian working there. Maria had an arrangement with Barraud, who had an arrangement with the Genevan police, whereby her two top trainees from her restaurant in Rio could come and work for three months in Geneva: it was a sort of prize. Wagner was grateful to Maria and Barraud, but this was not at all what he had thought that he had agreed to when Gregori had told him that he was going to be doing a course.

It was a bewildering time for Wagner. Maria thought it best that from now on he should be called Pedro, but that only contributed to his sense of estrangement; he hated the name. Wagner was free to move around at last, to control his own movements, to earn his own money, but he was now cut off from the people who knew him best and in a culture and climate which was the antithesis of Brazil.

'He was very depressed,' said Maria, 'devastated.' People scurried around to try to make him feel at home. A man from the consulate gave him a coat and jacket. Another consulate employee offered him French lessons. Maria and a friend took him out and bought him clothes at their own expense. To welcome him, Maria held a *feijoada* in her home – the dense, meat, sausage and bean stew that makes for a traditional Brazilian Sunday lunch. Her son, André, befriended him – they listened to music together. Wagner would come over after his shifts to watch television. Very soon, a sort of informal adoption had taken place. 'I liked him,' said Maria, with warmth. 'He's very good. He's very kind-hearted.'

But work was not going as well as she had hoped. 'He can't work eight hours a day. He was fine at the beginning, but he got very perturbed because he has that bullet in his head. He doesn't have emotional control; he doesn't have physical strength. He can't take it.' She qualified what she meant by 'emotional control': 'He bursts into tears. He's deeply sad that he has to live here – when I say emotional control I'm talking about Brazilian emotional control, because Brazilians don't have much emotional control. I'm very emotional! And he was very hurt – very hurt by Brazil.'

Wagner said that the first five or six years were very difficult for him, but that then he began to get used to it. One of the things that bothered him was how quiet Geneva was: 'I can't have silence. If it's silent my head starts to mess up.' He took to wearing headphones all the time. He was ultra-sensitive to the moods of other people – perhaps because of his own delicate mental state. He had the habit, when meeting someone for the first time, of ignoring them for five minutes or so, as if he were tuning into them. He found that Northern Europeans emitted a lot of stress, which was extremely wearing to him: 'Brazilians are more laid-back, more jokey. They treat everything with good humour. And here it's very hard, very closed. Europe absorbs energy. Brazil gives you energy.'

Maria took Wagner to see a neurologist. 'He was extremely shocked by Wagner's story. He wanted to see if there was any possibility of removing the bullet, but he came to the conclusion that it was too risky to undertake an operation. For better or worse, he was talking, walking. But he had a serious problem in his ear because the bullet was moving. The neurologist said that *maybe* one day it might be removed, but that he didn't want to touch it.'

Maria also took him to see a plastic surgeon: 'Wagner had a very big complex about the disfigurement to his face.' The plastic surgeon thought he could do something – the operation in Brazil had been very well done. Eventually, Dr Nassif was contacted in Brazil, and he sent over all of Wagner's medical notes – even then, he said, there might still have been time. But the operation never took place.

Despite all the precautions taken to sneak Wagner out of the country in secrecy, it was only a matter of days after his arrival in Switzerland that the *Neuer Zürcher Zeitung's* Rio correspondent, reporting on threats in relation to the Vigário Geral case, also mentioned that 'in Switzerland, twenty-four-year-old Wagner dos Santos … is trying to start a new life with the help of non-governmental organisations'.[14] The sentence caught the attention of Marta Fotsch, a veteran Amnesty International activist. She knew Wagner's case well: the Swiss Section of Amnesty International had sent financial support to him. Amnesty contacted Maria Bourgeois and suggested that Wagner might benefit from contact with Amnesty members in Switzerland to help him settle in.

Marta Fotsch was Swiss-German and did not believe in the 'slightly irregular': 'I was astounded. I had been working on Brazilian cases in Switzerland for many years – refugees seeking asylum – and I have a lot of experience with that. But never in my life have I come across someone coming into Switzerland in the way that Wagner did. From the start, it seemed to me that something was not transparent. I'm used to going through the front door of the Swiss Government in Bern. I would make a visit, they would give their approval, and I never had any problems. And in this case I thought: strange! How does someone in this shape end up in Geneva working right from the start in a station buffet? That's odd! The man is severely traumatised, he should be seeing a psychologist, and he should have a contact person who can advise him about his legal situation, his rights. I wasn't used to it.'

When Marta first met Wagner, 'he was simply happy to be safe, that he could walk in the streets without being afraid about what might happen to him'. His primary concern was medical attention. His right ear was troubling him – it was causing him great pain and was leaking pus. Marta was uncomfortable about his status – she found his dependence on Maria Bourgeois and Barraud very unhealthy. But Wagner was grateful to both of them, and she did not want to interfere. 'I didn't want to put anything in a negative light,' she said. 'But I would have done things differently.' When she saw his accommodation, it only reinforced her impression that his situation was inappropriate to someone in his state of mental and physical health: 'It was inside the station. Below him was the restaurant, the kitchen. He had a small, very dark room which was maddeningly noisy and smelt of cooked food and grease. He was severely trauma-tised, couldn't sleep – especially given the noise – and I just found it all wrong.'

Andrea Chiesorin was also worried about Wagner. She wrote to Amnesty in London. Wagner had the habit of ringing her every couple of weeks to let her know how he was getting on, then one night in January, 'he phoned me four times in a row between 1.00 and 2.45 in the morning. At first he said that he was well, that he'd just arrived back from a party with friends. Then, in the following phone calls, he started to cry and say that he was very homesick and didn't know how he was going to cope, that the culture was very different; he repeated this phrase several times ... I am very worried about the support Wagner is receiving. His ego is very fragile. He needs psychological, possibly psychiatric care, appropriate to his depression.'

In Rio, Elisabeth Sussekind heard mutterings about Wagner's situation in Switzerland: 'A version emerged in which Wagner had been abandoned abroad. Cristina Leonardo was complaining and said that she was going to sue the Brazilian government and that she had asked Amnesty to take care of him. And I personally felt very hurt by this, because I knew that he hadn't been abandoned. It had been very dangerous for us. But I never contradicted this version. I never said, "It wasn't her. It wasn't Amnesty that got him there." Never! Not least from a point of view of security. So I remained quiet, I heard everyone saying that it had been Cristina Leonardo, that Cristina Leonardo had asked Amnesty. I just held my own council, annoyed, irritated. But I left it at that.' Elisabeth was satisfied that 'everything had been taken into account: that he should receive medical care, people connected to Maria who were going to do things for free, that he should have French lessons. Everything was taken into account. It was much better care than if he had been in a witness protection programme.'

It was true to say that Wagner had not been abandoned, but it was also true to say that he was now an illegal immigrant whose fate had been placed in Maria's hands and that his entire well-being depended on her goodwill and that of his employer, Barraud. It was also fair to say, that, having passed on the problem, the Brazilian authorities immediately forgot about Wagner, and, for that matter, Maria. No one in Brasília or Rio was responsible for following up on Wagner's welfare. Maria was overwhelmed by the responsibility. By her own admission, she was frightened, and her relationship with Wagner was an emotional, not professional one. He was a six-foot-two twenty-four-year-old, yet she could only think of him as a 'boy'. She talked of the 'love' and 'affection' that she had demonstrated towards him, of how she had 'saved' him. Wagner gently explained to a flabbergasted Marta Fotsch, who had asked Maria about his legal status, not whether she loved him, that Maria meant well. It was just the Brazilian way.

And so, things ticked along, with Wagner just about holding himself above water until things came to a head around the first trial, which was set for 29 April. Wagner was depressed, but he had not lost his sense of purpose. He was still determined to testify.

In March, Maria went back to Brazil to see to her projects in Vigário Geral. She was staying at a friend's flat in Copacabana. One night, very late, Marta Fotsch received a distressed phone call from Maria; she had just been detained on the street by a group of military policemen.

'I was in a taxi,' said Maria. 'The taxi driver asked, "Do you have anything to do with drugs, madam?" I said, "No. Why?" "Because some cars are following us." Then they stopped the taxi. The driver was very kind, because he drove ahead and stopped and waited to see what would happen. That's very rare.

'Then the policemen surrounded me, all the cars, I was dying of fear. I said, "I'm a teacher." "Shut up, idiot! You're nothing of the sort. You're carrying drugs." I said, "I don't have any drugs, you can search me." They wanted to frighten me. One of them had a machine gun in my face. I said, "Take that rifle away." Then the guy said to his boss – I remember it to this day, I'll never forget it – "She called it a rifle!" Then they started to circle me. I was terrified. Then they left, without saying anything.'

The taxi driver took her home. She phoned a friend of hers who was an editor at TV Globo and he said, 'Don't talk to anyone about this. Don't talk to any newspapers. They did this to frighten you.'

Maria was convinced that it was something to do with Wagner, although she could not work out how they knew of her connection to him. She had taken care to keep her name out of any press coverage relating to him. In her phone call to Marta she pleaded with her not to allow Wagner to return to Rio for the trial. He would not be safe, she said. He would be killed if he came back. 'She did everything she could to prevent him from going,' said Marta. But it was not up to Maria or Amnesty whether Wagner returned to testify, but to Wagner himself, and he held firm to his decision. Marta, who sought clarity in all things, asked him to draw up some conditions for his return, and he did so. 'He didn't like writing,' said Marta. 'It was an effort for him.' Wagner wrote:

1)   *I agree to return to Brazil.*

2)   *I would like someone to accompany me to Brazil.*

3)   *I would like it to be Andrea, my psychologist.*

4)   *If the case takes more than two days, I don't want to stay overnight in Rio.*

5)   *I would like the press to be banned from filming me.*

6)   *I would like to stay the minimum amount of time possible in Brazil.*

7)   *If Andrea can't come here, I'd like her to meet me on the aeroplane.*

The Brazilian authorities had not given much thought to what would happen when Wagner returned to testify. Perhaps they assumed that he would not. In a conversation with Amnesty in London, José Gregori, the National Secretary for Human Rights, said that he would check with the judge in Rio that it was absolutely necessary. He offered full federal protection to Wagner in the event of his return to the trial, but wondered if Amnesty could pay for the flight, as he could not. Amnesty suggested that as this was a matter of Brazilian justice, it was a Brazilian government responsibility to cover Wagner's costs. The Federal Government had taken to the idea that Wagner was 'under the protection of Amnesty International' and shamelessly put it out officially throughout the world in embassy communiqués as one of their human rights success stories.

It fell to Marta to see to the practical details of his Brazil trip, not least to ensure that he would be able re-enter Switzerland without problems. Given the reluctance of the government to pay for even Wagner's flight, it was impractical for Andrea to fly to Switzerland to accompany him. In the end, Maria, who had now returned to Geneva, was the one who flew with Wagner: 'I went with him. I paid for my own flights. The Ministry never helped, but I came because he asked me to. Before we left, Pedro Bial from TV Globo in London called me. I was a bit frightened. I said I didn't want any publicity. But he said, "If you let us come with you, without showing him, you'll be well protected by Globo." And then my son, André, who had all these friends who played music, had a friend who had a little studio in Geneva. He said, "Mum, I'll take Pedro [Wagner] there, and we'll give the studio as his address." I said, "And if your friend gets killed afterwards?" "He won't. He's blond. No one will mistake him for Wagner." So we arranged it there, and Pedro Bial was true to his word. He blocked out his face and Wagner talked about the massacre. Then, on our way to Brazil, TV Globo was hiding in the airport. When we were on the plane, Wagner said, "I want you to show how my face has been disfigured."'

Wagner had asked for no cameras, and had not known that TV Globo would be on the plane with him, but he accepted the premise that its presence offered them security. 'Globo is a power, isn't it? So, because she was going with me she wanted security for herself as well.' He shrugged his shoulders, 'I was emotional. I was fired up with a sense of justice. It didn't particularly bother me that my face would appear, because it was just.'

Considerable time and effort had been spent on securing the judge's agreement to keep cameras out of the courtroom, but it was all wasted. On the evening of his arrival in Rio, Wagner's face was all over prime-time television.

19

Nelson Cunha

SINCE OCTOBER 1995, Brum and the prosecutors had been convinced of the involvement in the Candelária massacre of Nelson Cunha and Marcos Aurélio Dias Alcântara, but they were still looking at other suspects, and were waiting for their moment. The secret investigation was not quite as secret as they thought, however. A few weeks before the trial date, Piñeiro was unpleasantly surprised by a phone call from a journalist, Elba Boechat. 'Elba came into our office – we already knew her because she had covered the Daniela case – and she said, "I want to talk to you." We already had a certain informality, addressing each other as *'você'*.* She said, "Read this." "What is it?" When we read it, Filho and I, we froze. Why? She had had access to two statements which were part of the secret, parallel investigation, and I said to her, "You've got a huge scoop. We're conducting a parallel investigation, but if you report this you'll destroy it and we will probably never get to the truth. That means that Candelária will result in impunity." This girl had such integrity. She had a huge scoop, front page ... She said, "I believe in you. I'll keep quiet about it."'

* As opposed to the formal *O Senhor/A Senhora*.

At the beginning of April they issued arrest warrants for Cunha and Alcântara, and two others, ex-military policeman Carlos Jorge Liaffa Coelho, and still-serving military policeman Nilton Oliveira, but only three of them were taken into custody. Cunha got wind of the arrest and fled into the interior.

The case was about to go to trial. The prosecutors were prosecuting four defendants, three of whom they believed to be innocent, and one of whom continued to protest his innocence and had an alibi from his family. They had six further suspects: one who had been charged with obstruction of justice, three who were under arrest, one who had fled and one who was dead. It was all getting a little complicated.

Piñeiro and Assayag took the unusual step of securing the defence lawyers' support for splitting the trial. They would petition the judge to try Emmanuel separately and first and hope for a conviction. They could then deal with the other defendants later, and in the meantime establish what case, if any, they might build against any of the other suspects. Emmanuel's conviction was still far from assured. 'We didn't know if we'd succeed,' said Piñeiro. 'Emmanuel denied it. He had always denied it. But we had managed to find some evidence to bring in the others, and we believed that, when he realised this, Emmanuel might tell the truth – in order not to prejudice Cortes and the others.'

Cristina was furious. She did not like the way that things were developing. She had accepted that the kids had mistakenly identified Cláudio, and that he was innocent. 'With Cláudio, I believe that there really was confusion in the identifications …' – it was hard for her to force out the words, it must have been one of the slowest sentences she had ever uttered – '… by the children. The children made the wrong identification. But,' she said, speeding up again, 'I have no doubt that Wagner was right about his identification, unlike Brum — he and I have a great difference over that. Wagner recognised Cortes and Cortes was there. It's not what I *believe*, I am certain of it.'

The only solid evidence that the prosecutors had against Emmanuel was the eyewitness identifications, and the only eyewitness who was prepared to appear in court was Wagner. They needed Wagner. They needed him as evidence of the massacre itself, and they needed him to point at the defendant in court. They needed him to be right about Emmanuel, at the same time as they were planning, in a few months' time, to tell another jury that he was wrong about Cortes. Actually, what they really, really needed, was a miracle.

And they were, indeed, blessed with a miracle. A bona fide divine intervention, right on the eve of the trial. This was Piñeiro's favourite part of the story: 'The trial was set for a Monday. On the Wednesday before, a lawyer, Dr Israel, turned up — he was a pastor in the evangelical church. He asked me for a meeting in my office. He said, "You probably won't believe what I'm going to tell you. However, I'm here on a religious mission. You are on the right track." I said, "Sir, I'm convinced of that, but what are you trying to tell me?" He said, "Alcântara is under arrest, and Cunha is in hiding, and I'm here on his behalf."

'Alcântara was saying that he was not guilty. Emmanuel was saying that he was not guilty. And this lawyer said that Cunha wanted to give himself up. Obviously, it was an emotional moment! "You mean, he wants to give himself up?" "You must be wondering, so I'll tell you who I am. I'm from such-and-such a church. I'm a lawyer, yes, but I'm from the church."'

Cunha, said Piñeiro, had not been expelled from the police as had Filho, he had resigned. 'One version is that it was because he didn't want to work with guns and all that. Cunha was studying. He had become an evangelical Christian.' Cunha had been moved to come forward, he claimed, after reading an interview with the defendant Cláudio Luiz Andrade dos Santos in the newspaper. In the interview, Cláudio talked about how he had been called from home to attend a line-up and had told his wife he would be straight back. 'I arrived at the police station,' said Cláudio, 'and the only black man there was me.' He went on to describe the conditions under which he was picked out: 'After the first session the official said that there was going to be a session with blacks only. As most of them, or rather, all of them were white, I said, "How are they going to have a line-up of blacks only if there's only one?" Then everyone looked at each other and, in order to say that not everyone else was white, there was a light-skinned *moreno**, but a lot lighter. There was us, and then they put a civil policeman in who was even lighter. In the end they said that I had been identified.'

Cláudio also talked about his faith: 'The words of God are clear: those who carried out this evil, this act of cowardice and are allowing an innocent man to pay the price for what he did not do will answer at the Last Judgement.'[15]

In Piñeiro's office, Cunha's envoy explained, '"Cunha belongs to my church. He doesn't want innocent people to pay for what he did. Emmanuel is about to be tried and he knows that he needs to resolve this beforehand. He doesn't want to negotiate. He just wants one thing. He doesn't want to be held in the Shock

---

* *Moreno* – dark-skinned – describes anyone of mixed race.

Battalion because there might be reprisals from his colleagues. He would accept the Fire Service.'"*

The lawyer said that Cunha was prepared to make a statement in Piñeiro's office. Piñeiro took to the phone. He phoned the District Attorney, the Fire Service, the State Governor, Brum, the Civil Police *Delegado* and a defence lawyer to represent Cunha. The only person he did not call was Cristina.

Brum did not share Piñeiro's sense of the dramatic, or his religious convictions. He was a spiritualist; he believed that energies that shaped the world, and that evils such as the Candelária massacre occurred when the forces of nature were out of balance. He was unmoved by Cunha's evangelism and sudden crisis of conscience: 'When he realised that he was going to be arrested anyway (we already knew that he was at a farm in the northeast of the state) he made a deal to give himself up, whereby he would not be treated harshly. And the pastor persuaded him to confess everything.'

The meeting was set for 10.00 pm that night. Piñeiro's office was packed. 'By 11.00 pm we were wondering if he was going to show up. He turned up at around 11.30. I introduced myself – I introduced everyone. I did everything that the law demands. His statement was delivered between 11.30 pm and 4.00 am. You can see how many pages – how much he told. He said that he hadn't done any shooting. That the idea was to teach the kids a lesson.

'He only told us what we were already certain of. He didn't tell us anything that we didn't know,' said Brum drily. 'His statement was conducted completely legally. There was no bias towards anyone. The only person who wasn't there was

---

*   In Brazil the Fire Service is a branch of the armed forces.

Dr Cristina Leonardo, in order not to disrupt the statement, because otherwise ...' Brum was smiling a rare, broad, affectionate smile '... her style is a bit tumultuous.' He forced a straight face again, and said quickly, 'Although she is an excellent professional!'

Cunha's confession was this: he, Alcântara, Emmanuel and Filho had set out to teach the Candelária kids a lesson. That it had been Wagner who had confronted Emmanuel during the stone-throwing incident. That his own gun had accidentally gone off in the car and shot Wagner. That Filho was the villain of the piece. That Filho borrowed his gun to shoot Paulo and Gambazinho, while Cunha stayed in the car trying to clean the blood. That he did not know why Filho was looking for Ruço at Candelária. That after the first killings, Cunha had been so upset by events that he had wanted to stay in the car, but that Filho would not let him; only Emmanuel was allowed to stay in the car in case he was recognised by the kids. That no further people were involved.

Cunha was relieved to disburden himself of his secret. He had gone home after the massacre, he told O Globo newspaper, and 'when I got home I felt sick with myself. I showered for a long time. The next day I arrived at the barracks and heard the news on the radio. I almost died. I was frightened of my own shadow. I was so frightened that I didn't even turn on the television.'[16] His ex-wife and mother had shared his secret with him for almost three years, and his confession was a relief to them too. His mother gave an interview: 'I have been in hell, and Jesus saved me,'[17] she said. Since his conversion, Cunha had been an active charity worker, concerning himself with the homeless, and bringing food to street children in the centre of the city.

'Conversion is gradual,' he said. 'You read the Bible, involve yourself in social work with beggars, street kids, transvestites. Only after all of this and a sense of remorse in your heart can you take the difficult decision to confess. Although God had forgiven me for cowardice and fear, he still demanded something from me because there were innocent men in jail.'[18]

Cunha's confession was very neat: only one car, only four participants, one of whom – the ringleader, naturally – was dead. Cunha himself had not intended to kill anyone, and the only remaining witness in the case, Wagner, had started it all. Police searched Cunha's house and found a gun that had been used in the killings.

It seemed too neat, of course, but, as Piñeiro himself had said, it was the prosecutors' job, 'first to do justice, and second, not to permit that the contradictions help the defence.' Candelária was riddled with contradictions. Cunha's confession gave them a clear case against three perpetrators in Candelária: the massacre would not, now, end in impunity. It was sufficient for them. They would not mess with it.

★

On 27 April, two days before the trial, journalist Octavio Guedes interviewed Emmanuel about Cunha's confession. Emmanuel continued to deny everything. He and Cunha were friends, he said, but 'he thought that he wants to come out of this well. This is favourable to him, because he's a defendant who has confessed. His name has been mentioned a lot and he went there, confessed, and complicated the case even more.' He did not know exactly why Cunha had confessed, he said. 'I don't know what type of pressure he's been under – is under. Something like: "Confess and it will reduce your sentence, or maybe you won't even be sentenced, because you're the main defendant." I'm sure that he will be held in a Police Battalion because he has a degree.* So he won't be so badly off.'[19]

Wagner walked onto the plane in Zurich believing that what he was about to do would be extremely difficult, but that it would serve his understanding of justice. He would simply tell the truth, and everything else would follow. But he was flying into a storm of bitterness and controversy, and the confusion that it would precipitate in his mind would never fully resolve itself.

---

* In Brazil, convicted prisoners with a degree are given preferential treatment. In civilian prisons, they are entitled to their own cells.

20

New Suspects

Rio's international airport was packed with journalists awaiting Wagner's arrival, but as soon as his flight touched down in São Paulo, federal agents boarded the plane and escorted Wagner and Maria discreetly on to a domestic flight. They put a bulletproof jacket on him, and in Rio he was taken off the plane while it was still on the runway and driven to the Federal Police Headquarters in the city centre, where he would stay throughout the trial.

By the time Wagner arrived, Cristina was in overdrive. 'Tumultuous' vastly understated her reaction when she realised that the prosecutors were taking Cunha's confession as the basis for their case, and would be pressing for the release of Cortes and Jurandir. She was running around town demanding that Wagner be taken to identify the new suspects before the trial. She also wanted a re-identification of Cortes. She was brushed off wherever she went. She and the Civil Police Chief, Hélio Luz, sniped at each other in the press: 'She is not with the police, nor is she a prosecutor, she has no authority to complain!' said Luz. 'I've never seen anything like it!' responded Cristina. 'Once again, a witness is being discredited in this country.'[20]

Wagner himself was more concerned by Cunha's allegation, in his confession, that Wagner had been involved in the altercation with Emmanuel on the afternoon of the massacre, and that he had been arrested together with Neilton. He issued a statement of denial to the media, insisting that he had had not taken part in the incident but had been returning from the beach, and that he would clarify this in court.

It was all utterly overwhelming for him. He was home, but there was nothing he could do there to alleviate the misery of homesickness; he could not go out, smell the air, see the water. Andrea, always a soothing presence to him, was there, but so was Cristina, and, although he was deeply fond of Cristina, her presence was not soothing – even when she was calm, she communicated agitation, and she was not calm now.

Finally, the judge ordered that Wagner should undertake some photo identifications on the day before the trial. He was shown a number of pictures of men that he had not previously been asked to identify. He made one identification: that of Carlos Jorge Liaffa Coelho, who had been among those arrested two weeks before. Liaffa was the man who had shot him, he was sure of it. Wagner did not recognise Cunha, who claimed to have done the shooting, and whose confession precluded Liaffa's involvement. In fact, he went further and stated categorically that Cunha had not been in the car.

All of this was duly reported in the press. Wagner's name was buffeted about along with those of suspects who had not, so far, been charged with anything. The lawyers, *delegados* and prosecutors were all commenting on the content of Cunha's confession, on the outcome of the new identifications, on Wagner's reliability as a witness. Even the defendants were giving interviews from prison. In effect, the case was being argued out in the media long before it reached the court.

Wagner had been prepared to be vilified, to be accused of being a street kid, beggar and thief. But he had not been prepared for his testimony to be cast into doubt by the prosecution on whose behalf he was testifying. Before the trial he met with Piñeiro and Assayag in their office. They explained to him that they believed that he had confused Cortes with Alcântara, but Wagner did not believe them. He believed that he was being forfeited in an elaborate game, the rules of which he would never understand. He had returned to Brazil to try to restore himself some dignity. He was now beginning to realise that he was in the process of being very publicly humiliated.

21

Sonia

SONIA DE ARAÚJO's husband was sitting in front of the television, a beer in one hand, watching Pedro Bial's feature about Wagner on the news. Sonia was preparing dinner. He called out: 'Sonia! O! Sonia! Isn't this bloke your brother?'

Sonia had not seen her brother in about fifteen years. It seemed unlikely that he had just turned up on the evening news with a different surname. She looked at the screen. It was hard to tell if this man, with his limping face, was the little boy she had last seen at the orphanage. She had not intended it to be her last visit, but she had been seventeen and heavily pregnant. Life had simply intruded. It had always weighed upon her mind.

Sonia had never followed the Candelária case: 'I avoid bad news,' she said. 'It reminds me of my own misfortune.' But now this Wagner was telling his story, the few spare details that he had managed to carry with him through life: how his mother and a sister had been killed crossing the road, how he had been brought up by FUNABEM.

Sonia mulled it over – she was unable to sleep. She discussed it with a neighbour, 'Could it be?' But there were too many coincidences. Helpfully, the television feature had provided

165

details of exactly where to locate this protected witness. Wagner would be staying in the Federal Police Headquarters in the city centre while waiting to appear in court. Sonia hopped on a bus.

Wagner was sitting, waiting, dressed, ready for court. He had chosen his clothes carefully. 'He wanted to look good,' said Maria Bourgeois. 'He wanted to make a good impression to show that he was no beggar.' He understood only too well that the sympathy of the jury was more likely to be against him than with him. He was wearing a cap and a long coat, which served the double purpose of hiding his bulletproof vest and enveloping him like a comfort blanket. Andrea was waiting with him. A policeman poked his head around the door: 'There's a woman downstairs who says she's your sister.' He had a note with him. On it, Sonia had written the names of her parents.

Wagner agreed to allow her to come up, and it was Andrea who went down to talk to her and see her into the room. The thirty-something-year-old woman who might be his sister was fine-boned and pretty, her clothes were impeccably clean and beautifully ironed. They talked for a while. He had very little to go on, and then he remembered that his older sister had had a birthmark on her tongue. Sonia opened her mouth and there was the mark that he remembered. In any case, anyone who knew what Wagner had looked like before his disfigurement could see the resemblance. They shared the same set of eyes and cheek-bones, the same burnished chestnut skin.

'*Ai*!' said Wagner. 'It was ... emotional ... I don't know! It was strange. I had no strength to stand. I just cried and cried and cried.'

They spent two hours together. Mostly they cried and hugged each other and Sonia talked. None of it sank in except for one thing: Sonia told him that he had two more sisters. Their names were Vandinéia and Patrícia. He had never known this – the name Patrícia had cropped up in his memory from time to time and sometimes in his memory Sonia had been called Patrícia. There had been a hazy recollection – something to do with a baby. The name Vandinéia meant nothing to him. But, for now, he had to content himself with names alone. Sonia had not seen her sisters in fifteen years either.

Sonia's face, all elated incredulity, appeared in the newspapers the day after her reunion with Wagner. 'After such a long time we're going to go back to being a family,' she told them. 'This is God's doing.' It was a rare moment of pure happiness in two sad, hard lives. But there was no time for Wagner to reflect upon it. He still had to appear in court. On the same newspaper page as Sonia's smiling face was a picture of Wagner walking down a corridor with his federal guards, on his way to the courtroom. Maria Bourgeois was at his side, her face taut and strained. The expression on Wagner's face was not at all what you might expect. There was nothing of anger or determination or fear. The photographer, who had been hiding behind a pillar, caught Wagner glancing over. His eyes were swollen with crying. He looked like someone bereaved.

22

The Trial

RIO DE JANEIRO'S courthouse was a shiny beacon in the centre of town, an enormous twentieth-century rectangular block tiled with copper-coloured mirrored panels. From the outside it radiated modernity and enlightenment. Four statues lined the pavement outside, lending the building a little judicial gravitas.

If, on the outside, the courthouse was an optimistic building, the architect must have felt that it would be dishonest to encourage optimism within, where a warren of long, windowless, low-ceilinged, strip-lit corridors appear to lead nowhere. The floors were tiled black to discourage even the unnatural light from reflecting, and along the walls, one after the other, were the anonymous, solid, dark, hardwood doors of the lawyers' and judges' offices and of the courtrooms. In the corridors there was a perpetual and apparently goalless scuttling, mainly of tanned white men in suits and ties with briefcases tucked under their arms, their purposefulness contrasting sharply with the listlessness and resignation of the mainly dark-skinned people sitting on wooden benches, waiting for something to happen at one of the doors.

On 29 April 1996, a demonstration was mounted in front of the National Library, which stood a couple of hundred metres away from the courthouse. The long flight of steps was adorned with banners demanding justice, citizenship, land, food and an end to impunity. There were people who had been tortured during the military regime, or whose children had been arrested for political activity never to reappear; there were mothers from the poor suburbs, whose teenage children had last been seen being driven away by off-duty police; there were people who worked with the street children of the city; the relatives of the Vigário Geral victims.

People flowed in and out of the courthouse as if on a conveyor belt. The courtroom itself was packed with observers, journalists and cameras. Amnesty International and Human Rights Watch had sent representatives to observe the trial; members of Viva Rio were also watching the proceedings. The international press had sent correspondents, a fact that was interesting enough to generate several news articles. At Candelária, the resident street population were earning themselves a small fortune by charging seventy reais to journalists wanting a shot of destitute Brazilians outside the church.

A Brazilian jury was only convened in cases of wilful crimes against human life. It was the culmination of a two-phase process in which a judge had already heard all the evidence, and in which the defendant had already received a full defence. The defendants stood in front of a jury because the judge had ruled that there was sufficient evidence that the defendants had committed a criminal act and a jury must now decide on their guilt.

It had taken almost three years for the case to come to court. 'We had the task of bringing to justice a case that had international repercussions,' said Piñeiro. 'And we knew that the defendant might be acquitted and could walk out, because the defence were going to be able to exploit contradictory accounts, and probably we were going to be held responsible for not being able to secure a conviction in Candelária.'

The proceedings started with the selection of the jurors. Of the twenty-one potential jurors called to attend court that day, seven would decide the case. Their names had been on a list of 500 eligible jurors randomly selected by lottery and made public every couple of months. The judge, José Geraldo Antônio, pulled names from an urn and read them out. Both defence and prosecution might object to up to three jurors without explanation. Once the jury was assembled, it was a curiosity of the Brazilian system that they were not allowed to confer or communicate with anyone regarding the case, including each other. They would be sequestered for the duration of the trial.

The four defendants were brought in: Emmanuel, Cortes, Jurandir and Cláudio. But this was a formality – the prosecution and defence had already agreed that they would request splitting the case to try the defendants separately and that only Emmanuel would be tried today. Cortes, Jurandir and Cláudio remained in court, watching the proceedings from the defendants' bench.

Marcos Vinícius Borges Emmanuel stood before the judge, José Geraldo Antônio. It was part of the Brazilian procedure for the judge to ask the defendant a set of questions at the beginning of the trial: where he was at the time of the crime, if he knew about the evidence against him, if he knew the victims and witnesses and understood what they accused him of, and so on. Unlike a witness, the defendant had no obligation to tell the truth, and he might keep silent if he chose. They were standard questions, and normally the defendant's reply would be the same that he had given the judge in the indictment proceedings.

'The judge read Emmanuel's first statement, in which he denied everything,' remembered Piñeiro. 'And then he said, "Do you confirm your original statement?" And Emmanuel said, "No. I want to change it."'

The cameras flashed. All the lawyers, especially Emmanuel's, pretended to be surprised, although they had already told the judge to expect a confession. 'I don't mind telling you,' said Piñeiro, 'that I nearly cried.' The surprise may have been staged, but the relief and the emotion must have been genuine. It had been three years of anxiety. It was a distressing case, and one of those cases that could make or break a career.

Like Cunha, Emmanuel was also suffering from a late crisis of conscience. 'I would like to tell what happened that night,' he told the judge. 'I've stayed silent until today, but I can't take it any more.' He did not want to see innocent men go to jail, he said.

'At around midnight I was at the window, when Marcos [Alcântara] and Maurício [Filho] turned up in the Chevette. I went down to talk to them and I told them about the incident at Candelária that afternoon. Then Maurício said: "Let's go and teach them a lesson." I went back into the house, grabbed a police truncheon and we left. On the way we went by Nelson's [Cunha's] house and told him that we were going to teach the kids a lesson.'

Emmanuel was very calm as he recounted his story to the judge. He was flanked on either side by uniformed military policemen; his back was to the public audience.

'Near Candelária we picked up the three boys. Nelson had a gun. Alcântara too. We approached the children. Maurício put them in the car. I sat in the back. The car moved off and the gun went off. Nelson said: "I've shot him. This one's dead." There was a panic. We didn't know what to do. We went in the direction of the Modern Art Museum. When the car stopped we threw two kids out. Marco and Maurício took Wagner's body by the hands and feet and put him with the others. We thought that he was dead. When all three were out of the car the shots started. Marco told me to shoot as well. I took a gun. I was scared and tense and I shot twice at one boy who was sitting.

'We turned around and went to Candelária. We stopped near Rua Primeiro de Março. Maurício, Nelson and Marco got out of the car. They told me to stay. I spent the whole time with my head bowed. I heard a lot of shots, two or three rounds, but I didn't see anything. Afterwards they got back in the car; we took the Avenida Presidente Vargas and went to the Rio Comprido barracks. When we got there, Maurício collected up the guns. I think that Nelson kept one. It wasn't until the next day that I saw what had really happened.'[21]

His story was very similar to that of Nelson Cunha, and, in its essential points, backed up the assertion that only one car and four men had been involved, and that it had been Cunha's gun which went off, accidentally shooting Wagner.

During his confession, the other three defendants sat and cried with relief. 'I would like to apologise to everyone who believed in me, especially those from the Military Police,' said Emmanuel. 'If you make a mistake you have to be punished.'

The judge called a recess – Emmanuel's lawyer, Sandra Bossio, needed a couple of hours to discuss the confession with her client, and to wonder to the press whether or not she could continue to represent him.

At 7.00 pm the trial resumed. It was time to hear the witnesses. The federal police brought Wagner into court via the back entrance. The corridor was packed with journalists. 'I wasn't angry, no. Really, I don't feel angry towards them. It's just a fact of life. But if the law exists – which is all artificial – it should convict them for what they did. They acted wrongly and so ...'

Wagner sat at the front of the court in his huge coat and white cap. He wore dark glasses, as though to put a barrier between himself and the defendants, who were seated a couple of metres away to his right. Everything in the last three years had been pushing him towards this moment. It had been a fixed point: the moment at which he would testify in front of a jury and tell them what had happened. But it had been an illusion; the point had not been fixed. In the last few days the trial had been split, doubt had been cast over his identification of Cortes, he had been shown a picture of the man he believed had shot him, Cunha's confession had accused him of precipitating the massacre and his long-lost sister had turned up out of the blue. His horizon had fragmented into thousands of pieces which rearranged themselves over and over again, like the patterns in a kaleidoscope.

The judge asked Wagner if he could identify anyone among the defendants. Wagner stretched out his arm, with the palm of his hand open, in the direction of Emmanuel. Emmanuel sat, impassive. The judge relayed the questions of the prosecution and the defence.* Emmanuel, said Wagner, had been sitting in the front of the car and had turned and asked 'Do you remember me?' For two and a half hours he answered questions, describing in detail the occupants of the car: 'The one on the back seat was between 1.68 and 1.70 metres tall, weighed around 66 kilos,

---

* Brazilian jury trials are inquisitorial. Questions from prosecution and defence lawyers and from jurors are put to the witnesses via the judge. There is no cross-examination, as in the British and American criminal justice systems.

was light-skinned, he was wearing a blue cap and a navy blue shirt; the first one to approach me on Rua Dom Gerardo had a broken right front tooth and was wearing black jeans and a light brown shirt with blue and white stripes; the one at the steering wheel was mulatto, he weighed 56 kilos, was 1.68 metres and had a moustache.'[22]

But not all of Wagner's testimony was clear. As always, he struggled with his memory. He became confused about who had been driving the car, and later about whether or not he remembered someone helping him when he collapsed at the petrol station, and the press would have a field day with his inconsistencies in their morning editions.

Wagner left the courthouse the way that he arrived: via the back door in a federal police car. 'He was devastated,' recalled Maria Bourgeois. 'He put his head on my shoulder and cried for hours.'

★

At around 2.30 am, after three and a half hours of testimony by Colonel Brum, it was time to read the evidence. The judge had offered the jury a break, but they had not wanted one. They were not allowed to go home, and so preferred to get it all over and done with as soon as possible. Every fifteen minutes they were brought espresso cups of strong coffee to help them stay awake.

The drama was over. Nothing exciting would happen now until the public prosecutors and the defence lawyers made their presentations to the jury. It was time for the reading of the evidence – a part of Brazilian court procedure so mind-numbingly tedious, that even during daylight hours no one really expected a juror to take any of it in. In shifts, court officials sat at the front of the court and read in a monotone, heads bowed over the files, every single document submitted as evidence by the prosecution, then by the defence.

The lawyers and court officials struggled to stay awake. Members of the public went and stretched out on the narrow wooden benches in the corridor. The jurors drank their coffee. The readers intoned – right through the night.

At around 5.00 am Piñeiro stood up and addressed the jury. In Brazil, the material put before a jury in support of a case does not have to be in the form of evidence. It does not even have to be directly related to the case – both prosecutors and defenders work to sway the jurors' emotions. They are trained in oratory, and in their two-hour address to the jury anything goes. Piñeiro showed the Candelária jury two videos recorded of the children: the TV Globo piece recorded with Glória Maria, and the tape made on Andrea's birthday the night before the massacre. It was the only time that the otherwise calm Emmanuel showed emotion. He cried as the Candelária kids danced and sang on the screen.

'Emmanuel,' said Piñeiro, 'was the instigator, the planner of a massacre that humiliated all of us.'[23] Piñeiro referred to other massacres: to Vigário Geral, and to a massacre that had happened only a few days earlier in the Amazon, of nineteen members of the Landless Rural Workers' Movement. In his presentation, Fernando Fragoso, the prosecution assistant (Cristina had been called as a witness, and therefore could not represent the victims in court), also drew the wider context into his argument: 'In this country,' he said, '6,000 minors have been killed in the last ten years and only eight people have been condemned for those crimes.'[24] It was not just about Emmanuel, or even Candelária. The jury were being asked to salvage the reputation of Brazil itself.

Sandra Bossio's job had been made very difficult. Forty-eight hours before, she had been expecting to go into court to defend a man who insisted upon his innocence. She was having to improvise. She talked about Wagner's alleged mis-identification of Cortes: Wagner was sure about his identification of Emmanuel 'but he also identified others whom we now know to be innocent'. But, seeing that Emmanuel had now confessed, any alleged confusion on Wagner's part was of little use to her now. She argued that Emmanuel had only been involved in the shootings at Aterro do Flamengo, and that he should be convicted only of grievous bodily harm, or attempted homicide at the most. Everything that had happened at Candelária, she said had 'developed from a violent emotion provoked by an accidental shot in the car ... Emmanuel had been emotionally violated, and, as a man, could not restrain himself.'[25]

The trial finished at 11.00 am. The judge, lawyers and jurors all retired to the secret room, where the jurors would decide their verdict by individual vote on a number of questions prepared by the prosecution. It would be a straight yes or no vote on each of the questions relating to each of the charges: eight charges of homicide, and six attempted homicides. The questions had been formulated by the prosecutors. For each death or attempted murder, the first question was whether or not the defendant had shot the victims. The second, in the case of homicide, whether the injuries caused to the victim had been the cause of death. The third question – and this was the most important, as far as the prosecutors were concerned – whether the defendant had cooperated with carrying out the crime. The jury had to answer questions on the motive for the crime, and whether or not the victim had been in a position to defend himself. There were over 100 questions.

'There were various charges,' explained Judge José Geraldo Antônio. 'It's the judge's role to apply the sentence based on the jury's decisions. Some of those jurors made technically dubious verdicts. Some of them made the verdict that there had been attempted homicides and homicides. Others decided that there had been grievous bodily harm resulting in death – that is to say that the death was not the result of criminal intent but that they had shot merely to wound, not to kill, and that the wound had caused the death.'

José Geraldo Antônio was a mild-mannered man in his early fifties. He had not accompanied the case from the beginning, but had come to it after the death of Judge Maria Lúcia Capiberibe. He had been shocked by the Candelária massacre. 'I didn't know that I would be judging this case. Children killed in such a cowardly way – children who were there in dire need. There was no justification! It went against human rationality. Only a person devoid of any human feeling could carry out such a cowardly crime.'

The jury found Emmanuel guilty of eight counts of homicide, but only one attempted homicide – that of Wagner. At around 2.30 pm, after a twenty-five-hour trial, the judge came back into the courtroom and read the sentence.

'Given the indignation, the behaviour, which had pierced international consciousness, and that of the international judicial process, and from my own perspective as a human being, and within my own conscience as a judge, I believed that he should be convicted with the maximum sentence provided for within the law.'

In Brazil, a sentence of more than twenty years automatically assures the defendant the right to a new jury trial, and traditionally, to pre-empt this, judges tended to award sentences of nineteen or nineteen and a half years. José Geraldo Antônio broke with tradition and applied the maximum sentence to each of the charges. It added up to 309 years.

Emmanuel showed no emotion as the sentence was read out. He was having difficulty staying awake. But as the news trickled through the courtroom audience and out to the steps of the National Library, there was incredulity and delight among the demonstrators. No matter that the 309-year sentence meant nothing in real terms, it was the symbolism that counted. Symbolism was their currency – without it the lost and the dead were forgotten, which was how impunity flourished. Many people had believed that this case would never be prosecuted, or that, even if it were, the defendants would be acquitted or let off with a light sentence. Yvonne Bezerra had been one of the pessimists. Now, crying with relief and beaming through her tears, she told journalists: 'We managed to win! It was three years of anguish, but it was worth it. It was God's blessing. It shows that we're going to end impunity in Brazil!'[26]

In Brasília the President's spokesman told the press that the President did not comment on decisions made by the judiciary, but commented anyway: 'He's happy to see progress in the fight against impunity.'[27] The Rio de Janeiro state governor declared himself 'reassured by the judgement'.[28] A string of commentators, including Human Rights Watch and Amnesty International, welcomed the verdict with various degrees of cautiousness as a step forward for human rights protection in Brazil. While in Emmanuel's neighbourhood, Rio Comprido, a neighbour commented bitterly that 'Emmanuel should have been decorated, not convicted!'[29]

Emmanuel gave an interview to O Globo newspaper: 'The sentence was too harsh,' he said. 'I was convicted of all the deaths. They didn't take into account the fact that I only shot one person. It wasn't intentional. It was as if I had meant to do it; as if I was a cruel murderer.' He had hoped, he said, for 'understanding. That people wouldn't see an eternal murderer, who did this for pleasure. I hoped that they would understand that I killed in a moment of weakness. And through inexperience, because I didn't know how to refuse ... I don't know why everything went wrong. Evil really was operating at that moment and arranged things so that we kept doing more and more wrong, without knowing what was happening. My intention was just to hide, to stay down in the car. And the jurors didn't take anything into account. It's very easy to convict. Who does it satisfy? Themselves? The law? The NGOs? That's not how justice is done.'[30]

On 4 May there was a third and final confession. Marco Aurélio Alcântara claimed that he had not shot the boys at the Aterro and could not remember if he shot anyone at Candelária. At the Aterro, he said, Filho had ordered him to shoot the two boys, but, 'I refused to shoot, so he took my gun and killed them both. I couldn't bring up my son burdened with the pain of keeping innocent men in jail ... I acknowledge my guilt, but I hope that people won't see me as an animal.'[31]

And on 10 May, Cortes, Cláudio and Jurandir were released, to await their trials at liberty. But their names had already been cleared. They were confident that their trials would be formalities.

By the time Alcântara confessed, Wagner was already back in Switzerland. Before he left Brazil he had made a statement to the press. In it, he gave details about his other two sisters, Patrícia and Vandinéia, who had been living with a woman whose name he believed to be Jurandir Nunes de Oliveira, in Jardim Primavera in the Baixada Fluminense. He asked them to make contact via the *Centro Brasileiro*.

There was little relief for Wagner. He had not been believed, and this outweighed any grim satisfaction he might have felt at the verdict. His determination to testify had kept the case alive and resulted in a landmark conviction, but, as Andrea Chiesorin knew: 'On a macro level he understands that there was a positive outcome. But on a micro level, there is nothing in it for him.' Wagner was not vengeful. He saw the killers as victims of the same social forces as himself: 'They are also victims. They are. When you get right down to it they are victims. They are guilty of the wrong, yes. But people who are well treated, who receive affection, they don't end up feeling undervalued. And in the end they did what they did because they were undervalued. If they carried out their work well or badly ...' Wagner made a dismissive gesture with his hand. '...They don't have respect. There is no gratitude for their work. They do it to support their families, but in the end they find that however much they do they are degraded.'

For Wagner, there was only one positive thing to emerge from all of this, and that was incidental. In his bag was a Bible that Sonia had given him. It was the first present he could ever remember receiving from a member of his family.

PART IV

Exile

23

Understanding the Past

WHEN VANDINÉIA WAS thirteen she overheard her aunt telling her husband that her mother had tried to kill her. That was how she found out that she and her sister Patrícia were adopted as babies. They had often been asked, as they were growing up, how it was that they were so dark-skinned when their mother was light. They had always been told that their father had been very dark, and that they took after him. Their adoptive mother, Dona Jurandir, known as Mãe Dida by the people who petitioned her to intermediate with the saints, told Vandinéia that she had taken her away from her mother, who had been trying to kill her by bashing her head on the railway line. She also told the two girls that they had a brother called Wagner, but that she did not know where he was, and that their father had been a criminal and their mother a drunk, from which they were to infer that Wagner would be too: 'People who grow up without a mother and father are worthless,' she told them.

Vandinéia still looked like a girl, although she was a mother of three, in her thirties and had a streak of grey in her hair. She lived in the suburbs behind a roadside bar. Her front yard was studded with beer-bottle caps, and her living room full of the noise of men drinking. She was round and comforting and talked slowly in a bell-like voice, laughing frequently, mostly at herself and Mãe Dida. Patrícia was tall and slim, and not much given to sentimental family reminiscing. They had both spent their adolescence fascinated by their lost brother, imagining him to be bad and dangerous. 'I thought that every boy was my brother,' said Vandinéia. 'And I thought that every girl was my sister, Sonia, because she had left home and disappeared.'

They had followed Wagner's case in the news: 'The name attracted my attention. I became very involved,' laughed Vandinéia. 'I prayed! I said to myself, "My God, the boy has no mother!" I had a strange, bad feeling. Nowadays people tell me that I was sensing something.' Patrícia had felt it too – but less so. Vandinéia was the emotional one in the family. 'And I was always talking about it: "Patrícia, that Candelária boy's coming. Tomorrow he's arriving in Brazil. He's going to testify. And then he gave that interview to Fantástico, and we didn't see it. Then some relatives of my mother's came to the house: "Have you seen what's happened? Don't you know what's happened? That Candelária boy is your brother. He's your brother!"

'At the time – on the day, I became very depressed, because it wasn't what I had expected. I had this notion that he was a dangerous person. But I didn't think that his life had taken such a serious course. I left work. All I could think about was my brother. And when we managed to talk to him he had already gone back to Switzerland.'

It was Patrícia who spoke first to Wagner: 'Those basic questions: what he was like, if he was fat or thin, if he was good-looking or not. He asked the same of me: if I was studying, if I had a boyfriend.' He asked Vandinéia if she looked like Patrícia:

'I said that I though she was lighter; he said that he was lighter too. Patrícia is tall; he said he was tall too. He made a mental image of us, and we made one of him.' Every Tuesday they went into the city to the *Centro Brasileiro* to phone Wagner in Geneva. They also enlisted the help of a journalist to track down Sonia. When they met with her, said Vandinéia, it was 'a sea of roses'. With time they would have their differences – Sonia's life had been a lot harder than theirs – but the sisters' first reunion with Wagner when he returned to testify at the trial of Nelson Cunha was a joyous occasion. 'It was as if we had only been apart for a week,' said Vandinéia.

For three years, the requirement that Wagner remember had caused him enormous pain. His mind resisted the details of the Candelária shootings like a horse baulking at a fence, yet he forced himself to approach again and again until the leap could be made. It had been as if he had no past beyond Candelária, but now, with the reappearance of his sisters, he wanted to remember, to reconstruct his past. Memory had been burdensome to Sonia, too. She had been alone with the sad history of their family. There had been no one to share it with. In time, when the euphoria wore off, she would realise that she would always be alone with it – everyone else involved was either too young to remember or had died or disappeared; there would be no sharing; only imparting what she knew.

Over the next few years, Wagner would piece together his story. Sometimes, he would say, 'You'll have to ask Sonia, she's the one who knows all that stuff.' His mind would always, now, have trouble securing details. Sometimes they would be there, and other times the clouds hung across them. But it was, to begin with, a straightforward story, one shared by millions of *Cariocas*, and it started in the dustbowls of the drought-ridden northeast of the 1960s.

Sonia lived a short walk away from Candelária Church, just where the bustling, stall-lined street ran into the foot of the hills. In the lobby of her dilapidated apartment building a note read 'Occupants are advised that, due to the electricity failure, they may not bring visitors into the building. The Committee.' Sonia belonged to the Homeless Workers' Movement (MTST). The MTST was modelled on Brazil's famous MST, Landless Rural Workers' Movement, immortalised by Sebastiao Salgado's photographs of work-worn, leather-skinned peasants, tools held aloft, preparing to squat unproductive land on the enormous farm estates of the Brazilian interior. In the urban centres, the MTST squatted derelict buildings. The practice was often referred to as 'invasion', but Sonia always corrected the word firmly: 'It's not an "invasion" it's an "occupation."' She thought always in terms of class politics. In her window hung a poster with the words of Bertolt Brecht:

> *The worst illiterate is the political illiterate. He hears nothing, sees nothing, takes no part in political life. He doesn't seem to know that the cost of living, the price of beans, of flour, of rent, of medicines all depend on political decisions. He even prides himself on his political ignorance, sticks out his chest and says he hates politics. He doesn't know, the imbecile, that from his political non-participation comes the prostitute, the abandoned child, the robber and, worst of all, corrupt officials, the lackeys of exploitive multinational corporations.*

'The other day,' said Sonia, 'I was looking back on my past, and on my mother's past, and my father's, and on what I know about history – the history of people who struggle, you know? It all comes from our ancestors ...' Sonia and Wagner's parents were both the children of families who had moved south during the vast waves of internal migration that Brazil experienced in the middle of the twentieth century. In the northeast a fine terracotta-red dust covered everything, the beans withered on their stalks and the manioc shrivelled in the baking clay, while in the southeast the cities were building factories and putting up skyscrapers. Wagner's father, Francisco Ferreira Dias, was from the state of Sergipe; his mother, Ana Maria de Araújo, from the state of Bahia. Sonia did not know what her grandparents had done for their living, but what employed many of the men who came south was a harsh existence of hacking the lacerating sugar cane on the *Dono's* estate, or cajoling the herds of white, angular, high-shouldered, long-necked cattle across thousands of miles. At first only the sons left, but by the 1960s whole families were rolling up their hammocks, crating up the chickens, packing up the brightly decorated shrine to the household saint, and cramming themselves into open trucks heading for Rio de Janeiro and São Paulo. It was a long, bumpy journey, through a landscape of scrubby trees and red termite hills which grew rounder and greener as they approached the cities, where they spilled out onto the peripheries to swell the *favelas*.

'When I was born,' said Sonia, 'my father, he was in jail. Now I don't know what article it was for ...' Prisoners always referred to their convictions by the corresponding number in the Brazilian Penal Code: Article 157 for robbery, Article 159 for kidnapping, Article 281 for drug-dealing – it was as though the number distanced them from the crime. Sonia tried hard to remember. It seemed important to her, as though it might better illustrate what kind of a man he was. 'No,' she said, finally. 'I don't know the article. I remember that I went to the jail to visit him, there in Bangu. I must have been, what? Three or four. It was just the one time. My grandfather took me.'

It was during one of her father's spells in jail that her sister was born – the one that Wagner would see die on the Avenida Brasil. Her name was Rosângela. 'She wasn't my father's daughter. She was another man's daughter. And this man, I liked him a lot, because he treated me well. Nowadays I can see that for me and for my mother, he was better than my father. It was during that time that my father was in jail that my mother got herself this guy. But this guy, when he heard that my father was getting out of jail ... It's one of those things.'

Perhaps Rosângela's father cleared out. Or perhaps Ana simply went back to Francisco. She always went back. Sonia's fingers folded and unfolded on the tabletop. She always held her chin high, in a posture that managed to be both guarded and assertive at the same time. 'Then came Vandinéia, and they split up again, and then got back together – because my father always beat my mother and she couldn't take it and I kept saying to her, "Let's leave, Mum. Let's leave. Let's leave."

'And I had an aunt who always picked me up to take me to my grandfather's house ...' Sonia paused. 'I've been remembering these stories,' she said. 'They're such sad stories.' She took a deep breath and continued. 'And my mother, she was with Vandinéia. Now, my mother drank a lot that day, she fell on the railway line, and Vandinéia fell too. And the neighbours saw and there was a woman who said that my mother was beating her, wanting

… but that wasn't it at all … Nowadays, with reflection you can see that someone who's drunk, can't … you know…?'

She circled around it – this traumatic point in her life, the point at which, long before he was born, Wagner's family fragmented. The loving mother that Sonia remembered had been an alcoholic, and one day she was out with her three-month-old daughter Vandinéia, walking along the railway line, which divided the *favela* from the suburb, and she stumbled and dropped the baby. A small crowd gathered around her as she flailed around in the dust trying to pick Vandinéia up, but the baby kept escaping her grasp, her head flopping against the track.

The word went around the crowd that she was trying to kill the baby. Mãe Dida's house backed onto the railway line, and they called her, 'Mãe Dida, come here! Mãe Dida, come here!' Mãe Dida had never abandoned the story that Ana was trying to kill the baby. Now, too old to do much more than sit on a rocking chair in the shade of her front yard, her eyes pale blue with cataracts, she talked, intermittently yelling at the dog, her pipe and tobacco on the table beside her. She smoked the pipe when she wanted to know something of the saints.

'I left my room and went, when I got there: "Mãe Dida, come, there's a women beating a child here on the train line." I went. No one dared go to her. She had bashed the head of the little one on the train line. I picked the girl up, and then a sergeant in the army was passing by and the people said, "Sir, you have authority. Can't you take the child?" Because the mother wanted to kill the little one.' But it was Mãe Dida who took the child home. 'And then her father arrived. He arrived with a stick this big,' she said, holding her hands wide. 'He beat the woman with the stick – she was drunk. They were good-for-nothings. The mother would drink a cup of *cachaça* and give half to her daughter.'

Mãe Dida, a total stranger to Francisco, suggested that he leave the baby with her, and he agreed. Neither of them ever admitted that there had been a transaction involved, but Sonia always believed that Francisco must have sold Vandinéia: 'Money must have changed hands,' she said.

Ana was in no state to understand what had taken place. By the time she arrived home she was hysterical because she had lost her baby. 'My father had his bad side,' said Sonia. 'When my mother awoke the next day and was sober, he told her that Vandinéia had been stolen, and he beat her to punish her. That was a great wrong on my father's part – he had given her away. He'd settled everything.'

Sonia's voice rose. Brazilian Portuguese, so lyrical when spoken in a low voice, became querulous in the recounting of sad stories. It was as thought the language itself was incredulous at its own words.

'Then people started to say where my sister lived and I kept going by there. One day I asked my father, "Did you give her away." And he said, "Yes. I'll take you there one day." And he took me, and there was Vandinéia, fat and pretty, poor thing. Then I took my mother aside and said to her, "Look, he took me to the woman's house where Vandinéia is, but you mustn't say anything to him otherwise he'll kill us both." And then we went that way to go to the market – the market was every Friday – and I gave my mother a look and she knew which house it was.'

Mãe Dida had also adopted her oldest daughter, Jeane, although Jeane still did not know it when Vandinéia arrived. She was thirteen at the time, and delighted to have a baby sister. As a woman in her forties, her eyes still welled up each time she remembered the day that Mãe Dida took Vandinéia in. She wore a black T-shirt. It read: 'STOP. Allow me to identify myself before you shoot.'

Jeane too had witnessed the incident on the train line, and knew that Ana had not intended to harm the baby. 'She was just picking up her daughter any old how; she didn't know where her head was. She wanted to pick up her daughter, but she was drunk. The story that the mother was killing the girl is a lie, it's not true. She was drunk. She didn't have her reflexes.'

In the weeks after, Jeane would see Ana trying to catch a glimpse of Vandinéia: 'She paced up and down [outside the house], because she knew that her daughter was inside. You know those dogs, when they have a litter? That's how she was, poor thing. She wandered up and down trying to see her daughter, because her husband had forbidden her – her husband had forbidden her to enter my house to find her child. In the meantime, ages passed and little by little she managed to get as far as the gate. But my mother wouldn't accept it – it was her egotism. She had taken the girl to raise, and she believed that she was the mother and the other woman was worthless. And so we kept the little princess.'

Sonia and Rosângela moved with their parents to another *favela*, where Wagner was born, two years after Vandinéia, followed by Patrícia another two years later. 'And then after a while we had a shack,' said Sonia. 'My father lived in his shack and we were in another shack with my mother, and when there was a row we went down to our shack. My mother had a better nature than I do. She wasn't at all bad-tempered. She couldn't read or write – it was me who taught her. When she wasn't drinking she was very affectionate.'

Sonia was now twelve. She was an intelligent girl with an explosive temper, and she was at the age at which the children of the very poor start to look after themselves. There is an expression in Portuguese: *se virar*. It means to look after yourself, to find a way of surviving in the world, to subsist. It implies a good dose of street wisdom. Children could be seen looking after themselves all over Brazil – quick, clever, skinny children with things to sell: pineapples or Chiclet chewing gum or bottles of water. Sonia found herself work helping out at the fish or vegetable stalls in the market.

One day Ana turned up at Mãe Dida's and offered her six-month-old Patrícia. Her control was unravelling and Sonia was detaching: 'I was becoming an adolescent. I started forming my own view of life. And I thought that the life that my mother was living wasn't right. One day there was a fight between her and my father, and I was always on her side, supporting her, but then she always went back to him. She always fell into his arms again. That was the last fight that I witnessed. We were sleeping in the square, sleeping in the streets, going hungry.'

There was one last fight. Ana went drinking with a neighbour – Sonia had begged her not to go – and when they came back she offered the neighbour food. 'She took a plate of food and offered it to the guy first, and I thought that that was an affront. Me and my sister and my brother all hungry, and she takes it and gives it to this guy. No. Then I took the plate of food and threw it over the guy and I said to her, "It's not right." Then she hit me.'

It was late – almost midnight. 'That's the last time you'll ever hit me,' said Sonia and left. She talked a bus driver into giving her a free ride and went to stay with her sisters at Mãe Dida's. In the morning Ana turned up, distraught, and begged Sonia to come back. Sonia refused: 'I said, "I'm not coming home with you. I'm staying here. I'm going to get some schooling."'

Ana was unable to cope. She asked Mãe Dida to keep all of her children. Mãe Dida was indifferent – they could stay, go, as they chose. Only Rosângela went home with her mother, in tears that she had nearly been left behind. Now all the rest of the children were with Mãe Dida, including three-year-old Wagner: 'A skinny little thing,' said Mãe Dida. 'It made you feel sorry for him.'

'I thought he was sweet,' said Jeane. 'He carried himself with self-confidence. He was like any other boy: mischievous, he liked to play. And I remember a chair that we had at home – a child's chair – and to this day I remember him sitting in that chair, like a king sitting on a throne. You know, he didn't seem like a child from the *favela*.

'Little Sonia was a tourist. She stayed from time to time, because she was already more independent. She was more used to her own way and to looking after herself. There was no way to hold her and keep her here. And my mother didn't get on very well with her, because she was like that – independent. The others were babies, so my mother did what she wanted with them. She could shape their minds, their thinking: I have the remote control for these two here – you understand? With Sonia there was no way. But still, she stayed with us for a while, then she'd leave, then she'd come back. And then she went to live with a godmother, and then she came back. And then later she ran away from home, and then I ran away from home, because my mother was unbearable!' Jeane laughed, 'Un*bear*able! I'm not a hypocrite. I tell the truth!'

Wagner did not stay long in Mãe Dida's household. 'He was an innocent child, only my mother made things up about him. She really had it in for him. She thought that because he was a boy he was going to bother the girls. My mother didn't like male children. Today she won't admit this, but she did not like male children in any way whatsoever. My mother had a dread, a horror, of male children. She had a problem, you know? But the problem was in her head. He wasn't like that. He was a normal child like any other. He was an infant. He had no malice in him at all. But she makes things up. She's still like that today. '

Mãe Dida summoned Jeane one day and told her to take Wagner back to his mother. 'I was fifteen,' said Jeane, 'I had to obey, because she was my mother, wasn't she? And so I had to obey, didn't I? So I took him and got him ready. I put a little orange outfit on him and off I went.'

No one was in when Jeane arrived with Wagner, so she left him with his neighbour, Teresa. 'And that,' said Jeane, 'is where Wagner's story begins.'

When Jeane told him this story, Wagner found that he could remember the little orange outfit. 'I could see,' said Jeane, 'that it's not good to remember these things. It doesn't seem to be good for him.'

Sonia became pregnant when she was seventeen, and, after that, Mãe Dida would not let her back in the house, and she went off to live her own life. Vandinéia and Patrícia led a very protected life with Mãe Dida. 'Her daughters were not allowed to ride a bicycle because they'd lose their virginity!' laughed Vandinéia. Often she would ban them from going to school, because she would suddenly start to worry about exposing them to boys.

Patrícia, now in her thirties, went to evening classes to try to recuperate her lost education. It was her ambition one day to become a lawyer, tiny step by tiny step.

For a while they had someone they called father, but Mãe Dida eventually kicked him out too: 'My mother dedicated herself to her occultism, to her spiritualism, so she never had a husband. She worships an entity – there in her own mind. She carries out rituals. She thinks it will make her famous,' said Jeane. She left home as soon as she could: 'I grew up very bitter. I grew up very bitter because my mother beat me a *lot*. *Ih!* If she heard me say this she'd take a stick to me and I'd get two blows for telling lies. She says that she's never hit me. But I'm no hypocrite – I like her – but she was awful!'

Mãe Dida was gentler with the younger girls. They grew up with her and her saints. She received her petitioners in her 'room' in which she had a tiered alter covered in a white satin cloth, festooned with strings of beads and rowed with brightly painted statues. São Jorge, Santa Barbara, the Madonna Negra. Her framed Umbanda certificates hung on the walls. All around the room were pieces of paper, handwritten petitions for wealth or love or a closed body, held in place by glasses, black with the residue of drying out coffee. She could only read and write a little – she claimed, the writing was done by her saint, Santo Amâncio: 'It's him who writes it, with lovely handwriting.' At night he sipped at the coffee and answered the petitions.

She had been born to it, she said, in her northeastern accent, with its solid ds. 'When I was about to be born my father went up to a place there in Maceió where only the *índios* went. My mother had been in labour for three days and three nights. So Papai went there. The *índio* said, "Son, I already know what you're here for. It will be a girl. Now, go home and when the thing you have at home does this ..."' Mãe Dida held up her forefingers and placed one on top of the other, '"... she'll be born. And then you'll give my name to the girl." And my father said, "I will. What is your name?" "Jurandir."

'And Papai arrived home and when the clock struck midday I was born. When I was three days old I had a fever, and my mother had a fever, and when she came round she said, "Did you see a man with a plug in his nose." And my father said, "No." And she said, "Yes you did." (Because she was stubborn.) "I didn't." "Yes you did, because the man was here asking for the girl for himself. And then he asked me to give his name to the girl and said the same name that you did."

'The *indio* had also said to Papai that he would knock at four churches. In the last church the padre baptised me, but put me in the book as if I were male – because it's a man's name: Jurandir.

'When I was four years old I started having those dizzy spells. Papai said that I kept falling. I had never been unwell. And then Papai remembered. Then it started. The saint came. Santo Amâncio. Then I started to work.'

Patrícia still lived with Mãe Dida. Her house, at the foot of a green hill, with a walled front yard, containing a slouching dog and several cats, was a place where Wagner liked to be when he came to Rio. It was calm there. In the background cockerels crowed and water ran unchecked into the sink next to the front door. And at night, when Mãe Dida went to bed, Santo Amâncio would come and sit and rock in the chair in her room, looking for company, until she said, 'That's enough! Off with you now!'

24

No Return

WAGNER'S FLAT IN Geneva was modest by European standards. It was in a block of social housing, next to a busy arterial road. The long corridors echoed with emptiness, but they were clean and well-maintained. The flat itself consisted of one large room with some kitchen units in a corner. Paper was strewn everywhere, and there was a wooden Father Christmas on top of the television, which was always on, playing samba concert videos. By the standards of someone who had been born in a Rio *favela* and had experienced homelessness, it was very comfortable. At times there had been up to eight of Wagner's friends sharing his flat with him, sleeping crammed together on mattresses on the floor, but he had kicked them all out and was enjoying his quiet haven. When he felt like it, he invited people over and cooked them up a *feijoada*, but he did not like to cook for himself alone, and in the evenings was most often to be found in a Brazilian bar with his fellow ex-patriots. So far from home, they dropped their class distinctions, and lawyers, musicians, dishwashers and prostitutes all huddled together, unaccustomedly pale and encumbered by warm clothing.

Wagner's health would always be precarious. He spent time in a wheelchair after dislodging one of the bullets in his head during a fall. (He was trying to climb onto a roof to fetch a football.) The lead and mercury from the bullets were slowly poisoning him, but he had stopped taking all medication after a nurse administered the wrong dose of something and sent him into a fit. Instead, he played football every week, used the banjo as physiotherapy for his hand, took herbal remedies of some sort or another and felt much better for it.

It had taken many years, but Wagner was almost resigned to life in Switzerland. His strategy was to live there, under the cold sky surrounded by snow-capped mountains, as if he were still in Rio. He spoke Portuguese to everyone, summoning waiters with the jocular Brazilian '*Ó chefe!*' and succumbing to French only when absolutely necessary. He called on his friends by standing in front of their apartment buildings and yelling their names at windows closed against the weather, startling respectably hatted and coated Swiss gentlemen into turning and staring. He knew every Brazilian in Geneva, and navigated the city by restaurant kitchens, dropping in to chat with his friends and helping out when they were short-staffed. His sustenance was still music, and he played in the percussion group of a samba band. Everywhere he went he met people he knew and stopped for a handshake or a quick chat. Around his wrists he wore colourful Bahian ribbons, knotted three times to hold a wish which would be granted when the ribbon fell off. And around his neck a Madonna pendant, a crucifix and a *figa* – the Afro-Brazilian black wooden fist which wards off the evil eye.

On one of his trips to Brazil, he had had himself baptised. 'No one knows if I was baptised or not. My whole life I thought, how come everyone else is baptised? How come everyone else has a family? Now I've found my family and had myself baptised. I'm getting my life to where it ought to be.'

Wagner's equilibrium had been hard won. When he returned to Switzerland in May 1996, after the trial of Emmanuel, it had been to the same desperate situation of estrangement and uncertainty about his status. Worst of all, it seemed to have been for nothing. His testimony had not been believed.

Before Wagner had left Rio, he had been called to an identification line-up at the police station. The result was the same as it had been with the photo identifications three days earlier. He did not recognise Cunha, who claimed to have shot him, but he did recognise Liaffa. 'He looked at Liaffa for three or four minutes and pointed at him with conviction,' said the head of the Civil Police investigation, *Delegado* Jorge Serra. 'He had tears in his eyes when he pointed at Liaffa.'[32]

Cunha's lawyer was irritated: 'The identifications are faulty, in my opinion. Wagner was wounded and unconscious. How can he recognise someone who denies involvement, when my client has spontaneously confessed and he doesn't recognise him?'[33]

Cristina crowed in the press that 'this doesn't invalidate Wagner's testimony, but strengthens it. From the beginning he has been certain that Liaffa was responsible for the shooting.' As for Wagner, she said, he would not be coming back: 'He feels that he was disbelieved, that they gave no importance to what he said. He is hurt and does not intend to return to the country to testify at the next trial.'[34]

In May 1996, shortly after the confession of Alcântara, and the release of Cortes, Jurandir and Cláudio, the remaining suspects in Candelária were released without charge, including Liaffa, who Wagner had identified in April. 'That identification occurred three years after the event,' said the investigating *Delegado*, José Serra. 'The weight of emotion on Wagner, after everything he has been through, needs to be taken into account.'[35]

A few days later a gun was found in Liaffa's stepfather's house. Ballistics testing confirmed that it had been used to shoot Pimpolho, the eleven-year-old who was the youngest to die during the massacre. There was a brief flurry of excitement, but the *Delegado* quickly put a lid on it. 'I talked to Liaffa,' he told the press. 'He reaffirmed that the gun was his stepfather's. I don't believe that he's a killer.'[36] There was another potential link – his sister owned a taxi. Could it be the second car that the Candelária survivors had spoken of? It all came to nothing.

The prosecutors did not want to take it any further, either. It could only confuse matters. 'The test only proves that the gun was used in the massacre. It may not have been used by Liaffa,' said Maurício Assayag.[37] Wagner was useless to them now. The confessions made his testimony redundant. They were pragmatists. It was time to wrap this case up.

In September 1996, Amnesty's Marta Fotsch invited Wagner to come and stay with her for a short holiday at her home near Regensburg in Germany. It was hard for them to communicate – she tried to twist her Spanish into what she knew of Portuguese, and he now had a smattering of broken French. He asked her if she had a tape recorder, and walked through the countryside recording his impressions, to take home to turn into song lyrics. 'I thought of him as a poet,' said Marta, with a little laugh. He talked to her about the letters that he had received from Amnesty members while he was still in hospital: more than 800 letters from people all over the world. He had been amazed, he said. The first one had been in French, and months later someone had translated it for him. He would never forget it: 'Although you're 10,000 km away you should know that someone is thinking about you, and fighting with you. You're not alone.'

It was his first autumn in the northern hemisphere: the first time he had seen the leaves turn colour. It seemed to do him good. He also visited another Amnesty activist, Laurette von Mandach, 'I was stunned by his intelligence,' she said, deeply impressed by the objectivity with which Wagner was able to view his own situation. Wagner showed her the best way to set and place mousetraps – he had years of experience of dealing with mice from working in the orphanage bakery.

During their conversations with Wagner, Marta and Laurette continued to try to get to the bottom of his legal status. He had now been in Switzerland for almost a year and his situation was as opaque as ever. Marta wrote to Maria Bourgeois: 'I set out everything where I somehow felt that things weren't as they should be, but really not with the intention of criticising her or accusing her of anything. I thought that we both wanted the best for Wagner, and that the best thing is for him to become independent and self-sufficient.'

Wagner's health was poor. He was suffering from a lot of back pain and dizziness – occasionally he fainted – and he had recently been to see a doctor about his ear infection. The doctor was horrified that it had been left so long, and recommended an operation, but as he had no health insurance he could not be treated. Since his move to Geneva he had been working a twelve to fifteen-hour day, five days a week, for which he received, after deductions for board and lodging, 500 Swiss francs a month

(£200/US$400). The legal minimum wage for restaurant workers was 3,000 Swiss francs (£1,300/US$2,600). Ostensibly, he was undertaking an apprenticeship as a *Patissier*, but, in fact, he was washing dishes and cleaning. He was suffering from chronic insomnia as a result of the constant noise in his room from the station and restaurant below and craved somewhere calm, away from work. Then, to compound matters, he lost his passport, which left him feeling extremely vulnerable.

Wagner gave the letter to André Bourgeois to pass on to his mother, Maria, but he would not do so. Clearly, he knew it would upset her. Instead, Marta faxed it to her directly. There was no reply. 'Since then she has spoken very badly about me!' said Marta, but without regret. 'One day she phoned me up and the things she said to me! That I had taken everything over from her.' Marta's eternally youthful, open face disguised a core of steel. When she felt that something was not right she could not be swayed from her purpose.

By now Wagner was used to people – mainly women – occupying themselves with his welfare: Cristina, Andrea, Maria, Marta and now three sisters. It was a lot of female influence for someone who had grown up with 400 boys. 'There are a lot of women in my life!' Wagner would grumble, with a mixture of pride and exasperation. He was good at maintaining alliances with warring factions, but his loyalties were constantly being pulled in different directions, and, as Marta found, it was not always clear what he wanted for himself. He did not want to upset anyone, but at the same time he was growing increasingly unwell and angry in the position he found himself in.

There was a flurry of correspondence and phone calls throughout the rest of 1996 and 1997 between Amnesty in

Switzerland and the Swiss authorities, between Amnesty in London and the Brazilian authorities, between the Brazilian government and Brazil's representatives in Switzerland. Maria was very unhappy about it. She felt that her relationship with Barraud was being jeopardised, and that her own efforts to help Wagner were being denigrated. He should go back to Brazil if he did not like it in Switzerland, she kept saying. She was battling with her own health problems and could be volatile — making semi-hysterical phone calls one minute, and the next apologising for being emotional and protesting how much she cared for Wagner.

The second trial in the Candelária case was scheduled for November 1996. It was the trial of Nelson Cunha, the ex-policeman whose confession had been the catalyst for the confessions of Emmanuel and Alcântara, and had exonerated the other three defendants, Cortes, Jurandir and Cláudio, who now awaited their own trials at liberty. Cristina, unconvinced by the public prosecutors' theory that Wagner had confused Cortes with Alcântara, was still doggedly pressing for Wagner's testimony to be taken into account in the proceedings. But Wagner's testimony was now controversial and at odds with the line pursued by the public prosecutors. He still insisted that he recognised Cortes from the car, that he did not recognise Cunha at all, and that he recognised Liaffa, who had not been charged, as being the man who had first shot him.

The prosecutors did not really want Wagner there confusing matters, but Cristina's determination ensured that he was called to appear in court. Once again there was the question of the conditions for his return. Maria Bourgeois called Cristina, begging her to tell Wagner not to come because it was not safe. She wrote to Wagner from Brazil, telling him that he was being used by Cristina and by Amnesty, that they only wanted to make money out of him. But still, when he was determined to go, it was Maria who ended up paying for his ticket.

In the Federal Police Headquarters in Rio, Wagner met Patrícia and Vandinéia for the first time. Vandinéia had always dreamt of having a brother: 'And when Wagner arrived, the first thing I did was sit on his lap, and he started to laugh. I said, "I've always said that when I have a brother I'm going to sit on his lap." And we were crying and he was laughing! It was very emotional.'

Wagner also had a visit from José Gregori. Gregori admonished him as if he were a schoolchild. He had been receiving reports of his bad behaviour in Geneva, he said. He should not think that he could keep coming to and fro to Brazil like some kind of a star. The Federal Police, apparently picking up on this contemptuous attitude towards Wagner, charged his sisters for the water that they drank from the cooler. Wagner was immeasurably disgusted. He loved his country, but, one tiny betrayal after another, it kept pushing him away.

His appearance in court was a personal disaster. The prosecution would not back him up, and the defence made mincemeat of him. Cunha was sentenced to 261 years. After the trial, Cristina paid for twenty billboard posters attacking the discrediting of Wagner. He returned to Geneva deeply upset, but, once again, he had a present from his family: his sisters had found him his birth certificate.

Bit by bit, document by document, Wagner began to construct an independent life for himself. Presumably after an intervention from the federal government, the Brazilian Consulate in Geneva was suddenly extremely helpful about providing Wagner with a new passport. Then Amnesty put Wagner in touch with a Brazilian labour lawyer, José Maria Hans, who worked for an umbrella union* which specialised in support to vulnerable workers, particularly immigrants, both legal and illegal. José Maria had something in common with Wagner: he had been a student activist during the dictatorship, and vocal in his opposition to the regime. He had fled his native state of Minas Gerais because the police were about to arrest him, but in Rio they caught up with him. Three plain-clothed policemen assaulted him at a bus-stop and beat him until they thought he was dead. 'They killed me, only I didn't die. I woke up in the hospital and everything was broken – in my face alone I had eight fractures. I was completely disfigured.' It was not visible now. A Swiss couple, resident in Brazil, had formally adopted him while he was still in hospital in order to protect him – he was an adult, but because there was a sufficient age gap they were able to do so. They paid for his reconstructive surgery, and when he recovered they brought him to Switzerland to study, and there he had stayed. It was in honour of them that he used the surname 'Hans'.

Wagner, he said, emphasising each adjective, 'was living in a situation which I would describe as inhuman, sad, horrible, in a rich country. He had experienced a great trauma. He told me about the work conditions and the exploitation that he was subjected to here under the protection of the Brazilian Consul in Geneva.' It bothered José Maria enormously that he could

---

* The *Sindicat interprofessionnel de travailleuses et travailleurs*.

not remember the name of the consul, as if he could not fully express his contempt until he had said his name. The name continued to escape him, however, and instead he managed to pronounce the 'c' of 'consul' in such a way as to transform the word into an expletive. He was no less forgiving of Wagner's boss, who was 'no more and no less than the president of the Hoteliers Association of the Canton of Geneva! A very important post.' In that post, Barraud was responsible for setting the minimum wage of workers in the hotel industry, and there was no excuse for him paying Wagner the 'miserable' amount of 500 francs. Barraud, he said, 'humiliated Wagner day in day out. He had become Barraud's slave with the agreement of the Brazilian Consul. It was absurd! And all with the blessing of the Brazilian socialites – a bunch of old pains-in-the-arse.'

At the station restaurant, Wagner confronted his boss with the information that José Maria had given him about the minimum wage. There was a huge fight. Wagner was fired and his boss locked all his belongings in his room. Wagner moved in with a friend, and went back to see José Maria. Marta Fotsch had been hoping that José Maria would act as a discreet friend of Wagner's, she wanted to tread gently. But that was not José Maria's style. He took Wagner to the Director of Immigration, who, upon hearing Wagner's story, immediately provided him with a residence permit ('He made an exception. He was very humane. Because it's extremely difficult to get a permit here in Switzerland – Switzerland's a very closed country'). And then he sued Barraud for outstanding income owed to Wagner – successfully.

After the row with his boss, Wagner dropped out of contact for a while. When he reappeared, Maria, who still felt responsible for him, was at a loss as to what to do with him and sought help among her Brazilian contacts. While she was doing so she happened to be at the same lunch table as a young international human rights lawyer, Isabel Ricupero. Isabel was a Brazilian who had grown up on the diplomatic circuit where she had acquired an impressive array of languages. When she met Maria she had recently been working for the Inter-American Commission for Human Rights in Washington.

The Commission was a forum where citizens of member states of the Organization of American States (OAS) could submit petitions against their governments where there had been a failure to address a violation of human rights. It was not a court, but the Commission could summon government representatives and witnesses to formal hearings, and make recommendations for action, which might include making reparations to the petitioner. It could also refer cases on to the Inter-American Court of Human Rights.

Maria was looking for the kind of informal assistance that she had been providing for Wagner up until then, but Isabel, who was growing increasingly horrified as she asked more and more questions about Wagner's situation, felt that it was time that Wagner's relationship with the Brazilian Government was put on a formal footing. Isabel was a modest person, she did not make a lot of noise, so when she suggested that Wagner petition the Brazilian government for reparations via the Commission, Maria saw no harm in it and introduced her to Wagner. Later, when she understood what was involved, she regretted it, referring to Isabel as 'that girl!'

Maria was not the only one who was affronted by what Isabel intended: 'To me it was very shocking working on the case,' said Isabel, ' in that so many people were so shocked that I asked for reparations, because the only thing that they could think of was impunity. Because that's the part that nationally is so difficult. So that they can say that they convicted one or two, but the whole idea – someone actually said to me once: "Asking for reparations for a street child!" For me the shocking thing was that it wasn't just the government, it was a lot of people that I knew. A surprising number of people you talked to informally suddenly revealed this side. They were very, very surprised. You had to say: "He's a Brazilian citizen. He was shot by agents of the state! He has rights under the law."'

Isabel met with Wagner to see if he wanted to go ahead with the petition. 'I did three or four interviews. I wanted to do the interviews because it's important for the person to tell the story. It's very hard, I think. I hate doing interviews with victims – it's very hard for them. I thought it was very important that he felt consulted. For me, one of the big things is not the case, there was the fact that he could get his own apartment, that he could decide. I've always wanted to not intervene in his life, because when you have such a serious violation, a person feels that he has no control and I think it's something that for the rest of the person's life he feels that somebody else is deciding. In this case it was worse because he didn't decide. He was sent into hiding by other people. He was sent here by other people. He was in a job he couldn't choose. He couldn't choose his doctor. He was treated like a small child and I thought that for anybody that would have been hard, but when you've suffered a serious violation ... To me it was important that he clearly saw that he could decide at each moment. I tried to explain to him that he wasn't going to get rich. Human rights cases hardly every make any money.'

Wagner was supporting himself in Switzerland, but now that he had been reunited with his family, he was keen to do whatever he could to support them. Cristina's civil suit for compensation was going nowhere. He decided to give it a go.

Back in Brazil, Elisabeth Sussekind, who was now in the important role of Federal Secretary of Justice, heard through her contacts in the Ministry of Justice that Wagner was 'causing trouble': that 'he was not exactly a criminal, but that he was having problems with the police, that type of thing. I heard that. If it's true or not, or if it's prejudice because he was known as a street kid, I don't know.' However this rumour started, it persisted and was, inevitably, embellished, so that it was not unusual to hear people in Rio say that they had it on good authority that Wagner was living like a king in Switzerland on the proceeds of drug-dealing.

'The Ministry of Justice was very hurt when this rumour started that they were going to sue the Brazilian government because Wagner was abandoned and hungry and I don't know what,' said Elisabeth. 'Because the Ministry of Justice had taken all the steps that it should.' The most revealing word in this sentence was 'hurt' – 'magoado'. It was a word that cropped up everywhere in conversation. Many people had been magoado by their involvement in Candelária. It summed up the extent to which everything, at every level in Brazil, relied on personal relationships, on favours, on gestures – a system of getting things done that was frowned upon in highly regulated Northern Europe. It was a cultural gap, and Wagner had fallen into it.

Elisabeth was a thoughtful, discreet woman. She had sympathy for Wagner: 'Geneva is a very emotionally cold city. If he could have gone to Italy or Portugal or Spain, perhaps it might have been easier. It must have been very painful for him – very painful.' But still, the extent of Wagner's unhappiness in Geneva was a mystery to her. Many people understood it as deep ingratitude. Moving to Europe for free was perceived in Brazil as akin to winning the lottery. But Wagner was not there by choice, and exile is corrosive to the soul.

For people like Wagner's old orphanage friend, Guilherme, his desire to return was incomprehensible: 'He has the greatest golden opportunity to live his life there! He can come, as he does sometimes, once or twice a year to see his family. But where will he work here? Where? Who doesn't know him here? It was on the television, it was in the papers. The people are stupid, but not that much. Many forget, but others, no. From my point of view he's better off living over there. It's a First World country! The law works there!'

As Andrea Chiesorin put it, 'For many Brazilians, Wagner doesn't deserve to live in Switzerland. He deserved to die. He doesn't deserve to live in Switzerland.'

25

Doubts and Certainties

IN DECEMBER 1996, Cortes, Jurandir and Cláudio were cleared by a jury of involvement in the Candelária massacre. During the trial, José Muiños Piñeiro apologised to the defendants for his role in keeping them in jail for three years. But he was convinced that he had done the right thing: 'We had to make a sacrifice. They had to be sacrificed. But we made this sacrifice to prove that they were innocent.'

Piñeiro always insisted that Cunha's confession, backed up by those of Emmanuel and Alcântara, was the most accurate version of events. He found Cunha personally very convincing. He himself, as he mentioned from time to time, believed in God. He had a Roman Catholic, not evangelical, version of the Almighty, but he had been moved by Cunha's remorse and efforts to make amends. And quite apart from that, he was a pragmatist, as he had to be. 'I believe that justice was done – "believed" is wrong. I am sure of it.'

For many people, though, the Candelária case had too neat an end for such a labyrinthine story. If the killers only left at midnight, as they claimed, why were there people answering their descriptions looking for Ruço at 9.30 pm? If it was to do with Emmanuel's humiliation after his arrest of Neilton, why was it Ruço that they were so determined to find? Why did so many of the children report a second car? And was Wagner right about Cortes and Liaffa?

Brum never abandoned his thesis that there were two cars and seven to eight participants. 'We know that it wasn't only Emmanuel, Alcântara, Cunha and Filho, but we didn't manage to get to the rest of them.' Cortes, he maintained, was innocent: 'If Cortes had really wanted to kill someone he would have finished Wagner off at the petrol station. In reality he helped Wagner to stay alive. And this weighed in his favour when I made my report. It's not possible – if I were a criminal I wouldn't help him to survive. I would suffocate him. He didn't. Wagner recognised him because he had an image of a person, a face. He could have confused time and space and whether or not it was in the car. This happens in the human mind. If you're in a traumatic situation, you confuse time and space. You record an image – but at what time, in what space? This was a way for me to redirect the investigation. Happily it was an investigation that led to everyone being convicted.' No one had any grounds to criticise his investigation of Candelária, said Brum. 'If it hadn't been for the work of my team, the Civil Police would have got nowhere.'

There was a body of opinion which believed that a deal had been struck in which first Cunha and then the others agreed to take the rap for Cortes. Why, exactly, anyone would do that, no one could explain, but it was said to have to do with the mysterious codes that bound extermination groups together and the political pressure under which the public prosecutors found themselves. Cristina would always believe that Wagner was right, that Cortes had been in the car that night, and she would always encourage him to believe it himself: 'They struck a deal between themselves,' she insisted. 'Cortes had a higher rank. We don't know, because they say it was *extermínio* but we don't know how the group was constituted, who was who, if there was someone who gave the order, and perhaps Cortes was very close to that and he could have threatened to talk, so they made a deal. Cunha was there. He *was* there. And then he said that he had given himself up to Jesus. That Jesus had saved him. They tried to denigrate Wagner, to demoralise the evidence. And then Brum said that Cortes was innocent. He will die saying it. They came up with a story to get a result.'

Wagner's sister Patrícia tried repeatedly to gain access to the case archives, but was always refused. 'There's something in that case that they don't want people to see,' she insisted. Since finding out that she was Wagner's sister, Patrícia had become a high-profile figure in the *Carioca* human rights scene, acting as a spokeswoman for victims of violence in the *favelas*. Like Cristina, from whom she had learnt a few tricks, she ran around the city gathering up documents. In the evenings she was catching up with her education. It was her ambition to be a lawyer one day.

Wagner continued to be hated by many people connected to the police force because of his identification of Cortes. Thirteen years after the event there was still vitriol in Cunha's lawyer's voice at the mention of Wagner. Wagner, he said at length, owed Cortes and Cortes's family for the three years he spent in jail and the death of his father of a heart-attack. It did not seem to have occurred to him that had his client not taken it upon himself to go out and murder sleeping children, then Cortes would never have been in an identification line-up in the first place.

Cortes himself never publicly blamed Wagner. In all of his interviews he said that it was not Wagner's fault. 'I don't blame him for anything,' he said in a 2005 television interview. 'I don't think he even knew. The guy had been shot!'[38] He seemed to understand that the forces that put him in jail arose from the shambolic police investigation and the political pressure to produce a quick result.

As for Wagner, with the years, his absolute certainty that Cortes was there would wane. But for him there would never be the luxury of *knowing*. Either Cortes had killed his friends and tried to kill him and had been let off, or Wagner had helped to keep an innocent man in jail for three years. Both scenarios were equally distressing to him. It was a difficult subject to broach, but did he think now, with hindsight, that he might have been wrong?

'In the state that I was in, emotionally, I should not have done the identifications – the state I was in and the psychological pressure. In Brazil they want to do things any way they can. So if I made a mistake, if it wasn't him, then may God forgive me ... But ...'

After the 'but' there was a muttering. In Wagner's head Cortes was still in the car. And for people who knew Wagner, and knew that he was not a liar, there would always be doubt about Cortes's participation.

A psychologist might be able to explain what happened in Wagner's mind, if he was mistaken. It is, in fact, remarkably common for witnesses to make mistakes in identifications, especially if the witness is also a victim. With the reinvestigation of old crimes using DNA evidence, cases increasingly come to light of surprising mis-identifications. Rape victims, who have deliberately studied their attackers' faces in order to identify them later, have, with absolute certainty, accused a man, only to find out years later that it was someone else. In Wagner's case, if he was wrong, then it would not be surprising. The trauma, the bullets in Wagner's head, the way that the identifications were held, the enormous weight of expectation – all of those factors and more would have contributed to the way that Wagner stored, processed and retrieved his memories.

Piñeiro and Brum did not think that it was something that Wagner should worry about. If it had not been for him, they both maintained, the investigations would never have led where they did. It was entirely thanks to Wagner that Candelária had not ended in impunity.

In 1998, Wagner dos Santos submitted his petition against the Brazilian government to the Inter-American Commission on Human Rights. At the time of writing this book the case was still ongoing, and many details were therefore confidential. However, it had already produced two important results for Wagner.

After making his name with all the high-profile cases that he was prosecuting, José Muiños Piñeiro Filho was elected as Attorney General of Rio de Janeiro state. In this role, he was asked to represent the Brazilian government to the Commission. Piñeiro was a natural diplomat, and was delighted to have the opportunity to explain to the Commission that the Candelária case had been successfully prosecuted and all the perpetrators brought to justice. There was still the question of compensation, however. Piñeiro explained to the commission that under Brazilian law there was only liability if the policeman had committed a crime using a uniform, an official weapon or during an official operation. Still, Piñeiro had to acknowledge that this was an unsatisfactory response. When he returned to Rio he spoke with the governor, Antony Garotinho, and suggested that he might approach the Legislative Assembly to draft a law acknowledging moral responsibility and granting a life pension to the victims or relatives of the victims of Candelária and Vigário Geral.

'Governor Garotinho asked if I would draft the proposed legislation. The meeting was on a Tuesday. On Thursday we presented the draft legislation at Guanabara Palace. He signed it there and then. He called the President of the Assembly and asked for it to be treated with urgency. It was approved unanimously, and to applause! Applause! But it was not compensation. The law doesn't allow it.' It was something of which Piñeiro was very proud, and it made an enormous difference to the lives of the people who received it and who had been waiting for over five years for any kind of compensation. Wagner signed his pension over to his sisters.

Every so often, after another great tragedy, the Legislative Assembly tacks on another list of names. But it was also little more than a plaster. Ultimately, Brazil had failed to take responsibility for the actions of police who used their status to commit crimes out of uniform. And, inevitably, the lack of compensation to the victims compared unfavourably to a rapidly expedited compensation payment, rumoured to be 180,000 reais (£30,000/ US$60,000), to Marcelo Cortes for the three years he spent in jail.

Following this first step, Isabel Ricupero called for a hearing, and in 2000 Wagner was asked to go to Washington. Wagner's main concern was to have reconstructive surgery for his face.

His self-esteem suffered enormously from his appearance. He believed that his face frightened children. Andrea, as his psychologist, was also called, and was asked to prepare a report about his state of mind. 'He was very apprehensive about his statement,' she said, 'and very confused about what he should say, because he had limited time. We worked on remembering the events, which is what is most painful for him. Before the hearing he had to tell everything to the lawyer who was representing him. He didn't understand why he had to go through it all again at the hearing.' What was also painful to Wagner was that the hearing might decide to take action against Brazil, and he did not want that outcome – he had always hoped for a settlement. Finding himself symbolically in opposition to his country only exacerbated his sense of exile.

The outcome (which took several years to negotiate) was that Wagner was flown to Brazil to have the operations to his face, eight years after the damage had been done. It was now far too late to undertake the nerve grafts which would have restored full movement. Instead, muscle was taken from elsewhere in the body and groups of muscle in his face replaced, allowing him some movement. The operation was successful – the marked droop of his mouth was almost reversed. He was able to smile again.

★

'Did you ever feel that you were being used for political ends?'
'Always.'
But Wagner had no regrets about testifying. He had only one regret – he should never have left Brazil. 'Because I'm here and they're there.'

'You think it was a mistake?'

'It wasn't a mistake. It was a manipulation. Because really they played me, they manipulated me, they put me here in a manner that was unethical and immoral to themselves. They never accepted responsibility. Today my life is here. I like it. But when I think about it, I see a certain cruelty in it.'

'But wouldn't you find it hard to adapt back to Brazil after such a long time in Europe?'

'Ah! That's the problem. I know that I'll have to leave one day. But I don't know where to go.'

26

March 2007

In March 2007 I made a final research trip to Rio de Janeiro and Wagner and I planned to meet there. There were certain things he wanted to make sure I put in the book. It was intended to be a short, discreet visit, during which he could also catch up with his family and see his surgeon for a post-operative check-up.

In Rio de Janeiro's international airport the plastic chairs were arranged in rows in front of the arrival gate, as if before a cinema screen. Vandinéia and Patrícia had been sitting in them since 5.00 am, which was an hour before the plane was due to arrive. Wagner's new niece slept in Vandinéia's arms. Patrícia looked around every so often, wondering fretfully if the federal agents were here yet.

'There they are!' said Patrícia. Wagner came through the gate, chatting away with the two plain-clothed agents, a man and a woman, who walked on either side of him. 'Mauro and Bete,' said Patrícia, obviously with relief; they were '*gente fina*' – 'good people'. Wagner was pushing a trolley with two enormous suitcases on it. He did not look as if he was only coming for four or five days. He had refused to tell Patrícia on the telephone how long he was planning to stay, because he knew that she would make a fuss if it was for too long. Patrícia had phoned me a few times in London before my own, earlier, departure, with a note of reproach in her voice that I should have been so irresponsible as to allow Wagner to buy his own ticket, and a little hint of suspicion that I might be concealing his travel details. I was not, but as Wagner was coming to keep an eye on me it was my fault that he was returning to Rio at all. Wagner, in his turn, answering my calls to Geneva, deflected Patrícia's concern with an indulgent but impatient: 'Ah!' He held the traditional view that women were generally hysterical, and little in his experience had encouraged him to think otherwise.

As he came through the gates, all was clear. Wagner could never, ever come back to live in Rio. In Geneva he stood out, because he was black and because he dressed like a Brazilian. There he was biggish, but here he was just plain big. And his clothes, a set of nostalgic references to Brazil in the form of cropped trousers and tropical-patterned shirts and his trademark cap, with sunglasses set upon the peak, were what a Brazilian might wear in Europe, but no Brazilian dressed like that here. He was immediately recognisable. There was no way for him to lose himself in a crowd.

It was like any other airport reunion, except for the concealed handguns. There was a slight awkwardness – the harsh artificial light leaving everyone feeling a little over-exposed. Everyone embraced – the girls exchanging heartfelt cheek kisses with the agents. Wagner was beaming. For his sisters it was his first full smile – they had not seen the outcome of his last operation, and his face, only partly restored to him, was a new, much more expressive face to them.

The airport doors slid open, and there was that smell: the smell of Brazil, warm caramel, the smell of burning sugar cane given off by hundreds of thousands of bio-fuelled cars. Patrícia talked; a rapid fire of scraps of gossip from the world of the bereaved. Wagner listened contentedly, looking occasionally out of the car window, singing snatches of song to himself and sighing: '*Esse Rio de Janeiro!*' He said, '*This* Rio de Janeiro.' As if comparing this, the authentic Rio, with the pale imitation he always carried around with him in his mind.

The sun was coming up over the water, silhouetting the hills black. Everything glowed pink: the haphazard terracotta breeze-block shacks along the side of the road, the vultures perched on the fences, the sky, the smooth bays. The traffic swelled, surging towards the city across the bridges. The highways spread to six lanes, then the traffic parted again, joined, then parted. It crawled along the flyovers and underpasses that cut through the crumbling warehouses and the tall cranes of the docks. There was a brief glimpse of the Church of Our Lady of the Candelária squatting below the flyover, a patch of white among the grey concrete of the office buildings. The sky turned from pink to blue. Wagner was home – '*Esse Brasil!*'

The bed and breakfast was a tranquil old house in the hillside neighbourhood of Santa Teresa, set above the crowds of the city. The federal police had been nervous about the security of a bed and breakfast: they would have preferred a self-contained apartment in the *Zona Sul*. But they were content with the set-up. We were the only guests, the walls were high and no one could enter the garden without some very noisy dogs noticing. Patrícia and Vandinéia lay on Wagner's bed poring over a box of Swiss chocolates and talking through the open window to Wagner, who sat on the balcony, smoking a cigarette. Soon they were asleep with the baby and the half-empty box of chocolates between them.

Later that day there was a family fight when Patrícia surprised her sister Sonia with Wagner's presence. In her determination to keep Wagner's arrival a secret she had told no one – not even Sonia – that he was coming. Sonia was indeed surprised, and also predictably furious. She and Patrícia fumed in separate rooms. Wagner sat and fed the baby her bottle. Vandinéia, who hated conflict, cried gently and silently at the window. The federal agents tried to make polite conversation. Still, Wagner allowed himself to be content. Family fights upset him, but you had to have a family to have a fight. They would make it up in time.

There was one other upset on that first day. Late that night, Patrícia told him what she had known for over two years: first Nelson Cunha, and then Emmanuel, had been released from jail. It was the sort of news that had to be told face-to-face. He took it calmly, she said. He claimed to feel no anger. But it was what he had always predicted. That the men who carried out the massacre would one day be free to go about their lives in Rio, and that he would not.

Over the next few days Wagner took me to the places that were important to him, starting with what was the closest to being a home: the Instituto Rodolfo Fuchs. The building had been empty for about ten years, and for about the same amount of time the local government had been renovating it. Clearly, a lot of people were making money out of never quite finishing the work. A big sign across the front proclaimed that it was going to be a 'Hotel City for the Elderly'.

No one objected to our being there. Wagner simply announced that he was an ex-pupil and walked straight in. It was the first time that I had seen him enjoy the act of remembering. Everything was newly rendered and painted, but the old football pitch and the area around the swimming pool were overgrown. Wagner marched through the long grass, throwing over his shoulder, 'You're not afraid of snakes, are you?' Patrícia and the agents trailed behind him, suffering in the heat. 'Brazil really likes to throw money away, doesn't it!' muttered Wagner, and the agents shook their heads in disgust at the blatant waste and corruption.

Some of the former FUNABEM staff had retained their houses opposite the institute compound, and Wagner clapped his hands outside one of them until a woman appeared. Her face lit up. 'Wagner!' She was the wife of the last director of the orphanage. 'She has my photos,' said Wagner. We sat on her veranda and looked though pictures, Wagner laughing with pleasure. 'Wagner was a bit mischievous!' said Dona Rosilene. 'The kind of things boys get up to!' He was in three or four photos – a series of the football team preparing for a championship of some kind, and an earlier one, from the year in which he joined, of a huddle of cheeky, black kids all gesturing at the camera, arms and legs akimbo, with Wagner's fifteen-year-old face grinning out from behind a larger boy. Her photos were almost all that existed of Wagner's personal record. He had carried so little with him through life. They talked about whether or not the kids in the pictures were still alive as if they were talking about eighty-year-olds. The life expectancy of a FUNABEM pupil was short; so many of the ex-pupils ended up on the streets that Dona Rosilene's husband had been called to the morgue to identify bodies after the Candelária massacre. Most had passed through Rodolfo Fuchs.

Wagner received another warm welcome at the hotel where he had worked after leaving the orphanage. When she heard that he had arrived, his former boss rushed out to embrace him and to tell him how fat he had become. I began to understand what it was that Wagner was trying to show me: that he had might have missed out on family, but that he had always been able to inspire affection. His former supervisor took him for a tour of the 'ranch-hotel'. They had added Swiss chalets and a medieval castle since he had worked there. Three of his former colleagues emerged from a hut in a cloud of *cachaça,* and stood barefoot in the dust, swaying. 'Is that Wagner? Is that really Wagner? Are you the Wagner that went to the United States?'

Wagner was a returning celebrity. He laughed and laughed, and at least some of the laughter was relief, that he had been so easily recognisable despite the number of years that had passed and despite the damage to his face. 'You see how simple these people are?' he said to me. 'Is that what you were like?' I asked. 'Me?' he said, grandly. 'I never change!'

Wagner was always thinking about the next meal. He piled his plate high with 'a good' fried sausage and onions, or with 'a good' meat, rice and beans. We went out for 'a good' *moqueca* – the palm-oil and coconut milk fish stew that is the trademark of Bahian cooking. In the bar a group of friends had gathered to sing some samba. It was mid-week. The bar was otherwise empty. They sang and played, taking turns to improvise a verse and all joining in with the chorus. This was the Rio of the heart, the authentic one, the one that *Cariocas* missed so much. It had once been a city where no one thought to eat before 10.00 pm, but it had become more subdued. These days many of the restaurants were closed by midnight.

Wagner's sister, Patrícia, a beautiful woman, mesmerised one agent after another with her talk of extermination squads, *tráfico* politics, shoot-outs in *favelas* and confrontations with the authorities. One of Wagner's agents, a big bald black man with the wonderful name of Espírito Santo, and whose views on European sexuality were formed by retrieving deportee transvestite prostitutes from the airport, teased Patrícia that she would never find herself a husband the way she ran around town picking fights with people. 'If my wife was like you,' he said, 'I'd have to hide my gun!' Wagner did not like to hear Patrícia talk about her work — he disapproved of the way in which she exposed herself, and worried about her incessantly. And so the two worried about each other and bickered affectionately, Patrícia flinching at each 'good' *cachaça* that Wagner drank, and Wagner complaining about how irritating and distracting her nattering was every time her cellphone rang about some tragedy or other.

But there were rumblings of discontent among the agents. The question of Wagner's security was a difficult one. Patrícia had been able to secure federal protection for Wagner on this trip because he required a consultation with his surgeon, who had not seen him since his last operation. The federal government, considering their obligations to Wagner fully met, had not been prepared to pay for another trip to Brazil to follow up on his treatment. On all previous visits since moving to Geneva, the Ministry of Justice had been involved in the details of Wagner's arrival and stay. This time, he had come into the country for the first time as a private citizen. Still, the ministry had conceded the necessity for protection.

Every morning a new pair of federal agents turned up at the

gate, but with each day they grew unhappier about their role. Patrícia understood their obligation to be permanent, as the risk to Wagner was permanent. The authorities understood their obligation to have expired. Wagner was no longer a state witness, the Candelária case was over and archived. The official government line was that there was no reason for Wagner not to return home. Why then, wondered the agents, were they sweating in the heat of the interior, looking at defunct orphanages by day, and, by night, trying to dissuade Wagner from spending the early hours of the morning at a crowded concert in downtown Lapa?

Wagner himself appeared ambivalent. He resented the need for security, and refused to behave as though he was at risk, even though people occasionally recognised him, commenting within earshot: 'That's the Candelária boy!' On the other hand, he felt, although not as militantly as Patrícia, that Brazil owed it to him. Part of the problem was the type of risk he faced. It was not like a mafia contract. There was no threat from any specific source. Rather, he was at risk from any corrupt police officer at any unguarded moment, and Wagner had a reckless streak, which was why Patrícia was always frightened for him. Isabel Ricupero expressed it best: 'He testified against a policeman. There's no way he can live in Rio, anywhere. Because some policemen – they want to be able to say one day: "It took ten years but we got him. And if anybody has this great idea this is what happens. He thought he'd get away with it but he didn't." Wagner knows this perfectly well.'

The other part of the problem was the same issue that had plagued Wagner since his exile to Switzerland. The authorities persisted in characterising any assistance to Wagner as either a favour or a concession, which kept the whole question of Wagner's security in the informal realm. In a formal arrangement, negotiation would have been possible, in which the federal police's responsibility towards Wagner, and Wagner's responsibility towards his protectors, might be clearly defined. It was the age-old Brazilian approach – everything relied on the unpredictable nature of personal relationships.

After I left Rio the federal police set some rules. They were not prepared to offer Wagner protection at Mãe Dida's house way out in the suburbs. He would have to stay in a hotel in the centre of town and stop moving about so much. Wagner did not like the hotel they chose for him, or the restrictions they placed on him, and eventually, to Patrícia's horror, he dismissed his bodyguards.

It turned out to be the right decision. He rented a room for a few weeks, saw his friends, went to concerts and played with his nieces and nephews. It was the first time in fifteen years that he had moved freely around Rio de Janeiro. He knew that he was always at risk and that he could never move back for good, but, at last, he was in control of his relationship with his home city.

Before I left there was one last set of places that Wagner needed to show me: the sites of his attempted murders. We had planned to visit them very early on a Saturday morning, when the area was deserted, but Wagner had been up debating with Patrícia until 4.00 am and we did not get moving until 9.00. Candelária was much quieter than during the week, but still, there was activity, and both Wagner and Patrícia were nervous of attracting attention.

Patrícia had told me that when Wagner started to remember, he walked. It was why she did not like him to drink alcohol, because it made him dwell on his past, and then he would become upset and want to just walk. Once he had made her walk miles along the seafront, she said: 'The agents were so pissed off!' Now I saw what she meant. Wagner took off, striding around the forecourt of Candelária talking, waving his arm to point things out, and intoning parts of the Catholic mass. He stopped to look at the eight body outlines painted in red on the cobbles in front of the church, 'I was supposed to be the ninth!' he said, and started intoning again. 'There!' he would say. 'No, Julia! There! There!' and start walking again, singing snatches of songs to calm himself. 'Come on, Julia! Come on!' he said, marching across roads, down alleys. The agents were growing more and more furious – one trying to keep up with him on foot and the other in the car, and the more anxious they and Patrícia became, the more agitated Wagner grew. 'It was here, only I didn't come from here, I came from there,' he would say, waving his arm again, 'No – there!' It was impossible to keep track of what he was telling me.

He marched us through the city centre, from Candelária to Praça Mauá, then on to the witness house and from there to Brazil Central station. The station had changed; the route the police had taken him was blocked off. He walked through a covered market, packed tight with stalls selling cheap clothes and leather goods. Music was blasting out of radios at every two metres, and Wagner sang along to the songs. He was still singing along as we stopped in front of a low metal fence, one metre deep in rubbish. It took a couple of minutes to understand where we were. This was where he had been shot the second time. Wagner was singing along to the songs and talking almost incoherently, and then he stopped suddenly and said calmly: 'Interesting! I'm not even upset!'

I had often wondered about the psychological damage. Wagner had talked about depression and how his 'head gets messed up', but I had only ever seen the philosophical, immensely fair-minded man who was able to separate the wrong from the people who committed it, and accept with a shrug of the shoulders that any day it might still kill him, or worse, confine him to a wheelchair. Now, here was the damage, plain to see. Remembering like this, being in Rio – it was toxic to him. It was time to stop.

Back in the car, Wagner said, 'It's my birthday next week. What are you going to give me for a present?' Wagner had two birthdays: the date that FUNABEM gave him when they estimated his age, and his real birthday. He celebrated both.

'What do you want?'

'A banjo. You pay half and I'll pay half.'

I agreed, and off we went in search of a banjo shop.

27

22 July 1993

SOME TIME ON the evening of 22 July 1993 a group of off-duty policemen armed themselves with guns and drove to Candelária. It was to do with Come-Gato, the boy they thought of as Ruço: something he had done, or failed to do. Perhaps they were working to commission. Perhaps he had been working for them. Perhaps they were simply enraged with Come-Gato for bringing this contagion of unwanted, unwashed, light-fingered, glue-befuddled children into the centre of town. It may even have been as trifling an incident as a boy throwing a stone against a windscreen which took the tally of Come-Gato's offences over the limit. Whatever it was, a group of men took the decision to go out and kill him.

It helps, when planning to kill someone, not to be sober, so the men drank beforehand and they took cocaine. They climbed into their cars and drove into the centre of town. One of the cars stopped in a quiet street where it would not be seen. The men got out to take something from the boot – perhaps guns – or to prepare it for something – perhaps Come-Gato's body. And while they were doing this some boys walked past, and one of the men recognised someone in that little group as being from

Candelária. They stopped the boys because they were potential witnesses to whatever it was that they were planning, and because the boys could tell them where Come-Gato was. Perhaps they simply intended to scare them. Perhaps if Wagner had not hit back when he was slapped they would have given them a beating and moved on, but they put the boys in the back of the car, cocked a gun against Wagner's cheek and the gun went off.

That was a mistake. No one wants to mess up their car by killing someone in it. And Wagner was not their intended target – someone in the car wanted to take him to the hospital. But it was too late, so they waved to their associates in the other car and told them they would catch up with them, took a U-turn down Avenida Rio Branco and drove to the Aterro do Flamengo. There would have been screaming – seven people squeezed into a small car, blood everywhere, two hysterical boys realising that they were about to die, while the four men shouted at each other about what to do next – but not for long, it was not far. They stopped, pushed the cowering, pleading Paulo and Gambazinho out of the car and shot them in the head and the chest. They fired two more bullets into Wagner for good measure, and then they returned to a blood-soaked car and drove to Candelária. Some of them would have had blood on their clothes and their hands. The whole incident would not have taken more than a few minutes.

They parked the car and got out. One of them needed to urinate, and did so, quite calmly. It was an act of contempt. They knew who Come-Gato was and one of them walked up to him where he sat, surrounded by sleeping children, and shot him in the eye, as unconsciously as if he too were emptying his bladder. They then opened fire on unarmed children, who were running away from them. They shot an eleven-year-old in the back. They shot dead another four pubescent boys as if they were rabbits. Then they drove away.

Other people must have seen them do this: security guards, taxi drivers, people driving past, cleaners drawn to office windows by the sound of gunfire and screaming children. None of them came forward, and not simply because they were afraid, but because they were inhabitants of a city so socially divided and distorted by violence that it was possible to feel more rage towards a bunch of abandoned children than towards a group of adult killers.

In the years after the Candelária massacre, most of the fifty-odd survivors would die. The first was sixteen-year-old Barão: he was playing on a pinball machine in a *favela* bar when he was hit by a stray bullet during a shoot-out between police and drug traffickers. João Fernando was shot by a taxi driver while he was holding up a car. Romualdo was shot dead by police, also while holding up a car. A girl called Beatriz was last seen being put in the boot of a car by some men. Sergio and Sobrinho were killed under the viaduct which was their home in Madureira. Michel, who had been one of the witnesses, was dead, but no one could remember how. Tiago, who had been Turinha's 'boy', died of AIDS.

And so on.

It is now impossible to talk about Candelária without also talking about Bus 174. On 12 June 2000, a young man called Sandro do Nascimento took a bus hostage. Some TV Globo cameras were in the vicinity, and pretty soon the whole incident was being played out live on national television: the drug-induced mania of the hostage-taker, the terror of the hostages, the deployment of masses of Military Police shock troops, the hundreds of spectators. Realising that he had the full attention of the media, Sandro began to perform for them. It turned out that he was a Candelária survivor. In 2004, José Padilha turned the footage into a brilliant, excoriating documentary film,[39] pitting footage of the incident against a biography of Sandro's life. There were parallels with Wagner's life: he had seen his mother die, shot dead in front of him. He had been abandoned by his family, and had ended up at Candelária.

The hostage-taking incident lasted four and a half hours. Finally, Sandro gave himself up. He came out of the bus with his gun to the head of a hostage, a woman called Geisa Firmo Gonçalves. A trigger-happy policeman fired at him and Sandro fired his gun. Geisa was killed. The bystanders turned into a lynch mob and surged forward. Sandro was bundled into a car by policeman, and arrived at his destination dead. Ballistics later showed that Geisa had been killed, not by Sandro, but by the policeman.

And on 26 September 2000, Elisabeth Cristina Borges de Oliveira Maia – Beth Gorda – was shot dead on her doorstep. She had recently testified to the Inter-American Commission on Human Rights during their hearing of the Candelária Petition. The murder was put down to her drug-trafficking activities, and it would have been a plausible explanation, but for the two wreaths of flowers that were sent by the two local drug faction leaders: a signal, people said, that they had not ordered the killing. To Beth's grandmother it was an irrelevance. She refused to accept the flowers.

Of the fifty-odd survivors of the massacre, twenty-six were already known to be dead by 2000, according to an article published in the *Correio Braziliense* in December of that year.[40] By 2007, TV Globo, in a programme about the case, reported that of the sixty-five kids at Candelária on the night of the massacre, forty-three had died violently, mainly at the hands of drug traffickers or extermination groups, another five had died of AIDS-related illnesses; of the survivors, ten – including Beth's Rogeirinho – were in jail and the whereabouts of rest were unknown.[41]

In June 2002, Colonel Brum started an investigation that he had never imagined he would have to undertake: the murder of his oldest son, Valmir Alves Brum Júnior, on his doorstep in São Paulo. Brum maintains that his son's death had nothing to do with his work.

In 2005, Nelson Cunha was released from jail, having served a nine-year sentence. No one noticed, except for Patrícia, who knew every bit of gossip in Rio. How had she found out? 'A friend of mine's mother is friends with his mother,' she said simply. Rio de Janeiro was a city of six million people, but it rarely felt like it. Emmanuel was released the following year. Alcântara, who never appealed against his sentence, was still in jail.

When Wagner talked the words 'survive' and 'survival' came up over and over again. He always used it intransitively. In his vocabulary you did not survive some*thing*, you survived as a mode of existence. He still believed in justice: 'Justice comes from inside a human being. The heart of a human being is self-respect.'

Everything in Wagner's life had pushed him towards another fate – the fate of a Come-Gato or a Sandro – but he had always been guided by a sense of right and wrong. His *Orixá* was Ogum, he said, who was represented by Saint George. He was always depicted with a weapon, the spirit of war. But for Wagner he was first and foremost the spirit of justice.

In all the pages and pages of newspaper articles about Candelária and all the hours of interviews recorded for this book, I looked hard for the word 'courageous', but it came up only twice: Piñeiro used it, and so did Elisabeth Sussekind, who also used the word 'noble'. Wagner's life, like others of his class, was a constant battle against invisibility. That was his triumph: he refused to disappear.

28

This Rio de Janeiro

IT WAS MY last day in Rio. Wagner and I sat on the balcony looking
out over the stone balustrade and the terracotta-tiled roofs towards
Guanabara Bay. Wagner fetched a couple more beers from the
fridge and lit up a cigarette. He was wearing only shorts and flip-
flops. On his body was the map of his life: the burn on his hand
from when his father set fire to the house, the line on his stomach
where his foster mother attacked him with scissors, the dark wine-
coloured blotches on his torso where the bullets entered and
exited, the scars on his wrists from his attempted suicide, the
permanent slight droop of his right eye and cheek.

Bougainvillia spilt over the garden walls. Ferns shivered
gently. A sprinkler whirred quietly on the lawn. Three or four
shots sounded below us cursorily – *pap, pap, pap, pap* – dry and
hollow.

'Shots,' said Wagner, conversationally.

'Strange time for it – mid-afternoon!'

'Just someone emptying out his gun.'

We sipped our beer. Sugar Loaf Mountain shimmered in the
sunlight bouncing off the bay. An undulating V of birds flew
across the sky.

'Look how lovely – the birds!' said Wagner, pointing.

'You have a samba for everything,' I said. 'Is there a samba to describe you?'

It was a corny question, a writer's artifice. But he had obviously already given this some consideration because he answered without hesitation.

'"*Menino de Pé no Chão*". It's a song by Neguinho da Beija-Flor.'

He looked to see if I knew who Neguinho da Beija-Flor was, but he had long given up being frustrated by my ignorance about samba.

He drummed his fingers on his thighs and began to sing. In his head he could hear the banjos, clavequins, guitars, the whole percussion group, a burst of sound, like handfuls of confetti thrown into the air – each tiny element turning at a different pace and rhythm, but the whole an explosion of joy and colour – and over the top the booming, deep voice of Neguinho:

> *Sou menino de pé no chão*
> *Eu sou menino, eu sou*
>
> *Sou menino pobre da favela*
> *Perambulando no asfalto*
> *Mas sempre fui um sonhador*
> *Olha seu moço eu sou um rapaz decente*
> *E mal visto mos olhos de muita gente*
> *De muita gente eu sou*[42]

It was a song about a poor boy who was looked down upon, but was a dreamer and wanted to learn to read and write to help his mother and little brothers and sisters. The words were a little on the mawkish side, but the tune, even without the band and in Wagner's thin voice, was light-hearted. That's what samba does. It lightens, leavens, mitigates. It's as yeast to bread, as salt to meat.

Wagner lost himself a little in the later verses and pottered about a bit in the song, going back on himself, and humming in the gaps. Eventually he ground to a halt. '*Pé no chão*' – 'feet on the ground,' he said, 'because in Brazil poor people's feet are always bare or in flip-flops, but it also means that you are firm about things.'

'We have a similar expression in English,' I said. 'It would make a good Brazilian title for the book.'

Wagner liked that idea. 'I'd have to ask Neguinho. I'll get Patrícia to do it.'

We sat and drank and perspired in the afternoon heat. Below us was this Rio de Janeiro, this beautiful, ugly, warm-hearted, callous, sad, joyful Rio de Janeiro. Above us the birds flew towards the northern summer.

Appendix

Candelária victims

Paulo Roberto de Oliveira, 'Pimpolho', 11
Anderson Thomé Pereira, 'Caolha', 13
Marcelo Cândido de Jesus, 'Careca', 14
Valdevino Miguel de Almeida, 14
'Gambazinho', 17
Leandro Santos da Conceição, 15
Paulo José da Silva, 18
Marcos Antônio Alves da Silva, 'Come-Gato'/'Ruço', 20

Convictions in the Candelária case

Marcos Vinícius Borges Emmanuel

Sentenced to 309 years, reduced at retrial to eighty-nine years. The public prosecutors appealed against the reduction and he was tried again and received a sentence of 300 years imprisonment. In Brazil, regardless of the length of sentence, prisoners can only serve a maximum of thirty years in jail, and most prisoners are released after serving a third of their sentence. He was released in 2006.

Nelson Oliveira dos Santos Cunha

Sentenced to 261 years. At retrial he was acquitted of all counts of murder and received an eighteen-year sentence for the attempted murder of Wagner dos Santos. He was released in 2005.

Marco Aurélio Dias Alcântara

Sentenced to 204 years. None of the individual sentences for the various murders was longer than twenty years so he has no automatic right to a retrial.

Bibliography

Amnesty International, *The Candelária Trial: A Small Wedge in the Fortress of Impunity*, AMR 19/02/1996

Amnesty International, *Candelária and Vigário Geral: Justice at a Snail's Pace*, AMR, 19/11/1997.

Bezerra de Mello, Yvonne (1993) *As Ovelhas Desgarradas e seus Algozes: A Geração Perdida nas Ruas,* Editora Civilização Brasileira, Rio de Janeiro

Dollinger, Jacob and Rosenn, Keith (Eds) (1992) *A Panorama of Brazilian Law*, University of Miami North-South Centre, Florida

Heaton-Armstrong, Shepherd and Wolchover (Eds) (1999) *Analysing Witness Testimony: A Guide for Legal Practitioners and Other Professionals*, Blackstone Press Ltd, London

Heaton-Armstrong, Shepherd, Gudjonsson and Wolchover (Eds) (2006) *Witness Testimony: Psychological, Investigative and Evidential Perspectives*, Oxford University Press, London

Neate, Patrick and Platt, Damian (2006) *Culture is Our Weapon: Afro-reggae in the Favelas of Rio*, Latin America Bureau, London, 2006.

Skidmore, Thomas E (1999) *Brazil: Five Centuries of Change*, Oxford University Press, London

Soares, Luiz Eduardo (1996) *Violência e Política no Rio de Janeiro*, ISER, Rio de Janeiro

Telles, Edward E (2004) *Race in Another America: The Significance of Skin Colour in Brazil,* Princeton University Press, New Jersey

Ventura, Zuenis (1994) *Cidade Partida*, Companhia das Letras

Von Mandach, Laura (2000) *Recht und Gewalt: Eine Empirische Untersuchung zur Strafverfolgung in Brasilien,* Verlag für Entwicklungspolitick, Saarbrücken

Documentary and Film:

Bus 174, Directed by José Padilha, Zazen Productions, 2002

Kriegerin des Lichts: Yvonne Bezerra de Mello und ihre Arbeit mit den Straßenkindern von Rio, Directed by Monika Treut, Hyena Films, 2001

Linha Direta – Justiça: Chacina da Candelária, Directed by Monica Marques and Danielle Ferreira, TV Globo, 2005

Shadows on the Streets, Directed by Darren Bender, Channel 4, 1996.

Paiva, Lúcio, *Wagner dos Santos*, unpublished documents

Endnotes

1. Ventura, Zuenir (1994) *Cidade Partida*, Companhia das Letras
2. *Shadows on the Streets,* directed by Darren Bender (1996), Channel 4
3. Mello, Yvonne Bezerra de (1993) *As Ovelhas Desgarradas e seus Algozes: A Geração Perdida nas Ruas*, Civilização Brasileira
4. Carlos de Faria, Antonio, Aniversário de crianças *Folha de São Paulo* (23 July 1994)
5. *Linha Direta – Justiça: Chacina da Candelária* (2006), TV Globo
6. As above
7. *O Dia* (27 July 1993)
8. See 5
9. Neate, Patrick and Platt, Damian (2006)*Culture is our weapon*, Latin America Bureau
10. Ventura, Zuenir (1994) *Cidade Partida*, Companhia das Letras
11. Lemos, Antonina, 'Sobrevivente arruma emprego e deixa o Rio', *Folha de São Paulo* (24 October 1994)
12. See 2
13. 'Testemunha da Candelária tenta suicídio', *Folha de São Paulo* (22 September 1995)
14. '"Friedenshaus" in Rio schliesst wegen Drohungen', *Neuer Zürcher Zeitung* (28 November 1995)
15. Guedes, Octavio, interview with Cláudio dos Santos, *O Dia* (18 April 1996)
16. Nunes, Angelina, interview with Nelson Cunha, *O Globo* (4 May 1996)
17. Nunes, Angelina, interview with Theresa Avelina de Oliveira, *O Globo* (28 April 1996)
18. See 16
19. Guedes, Octavio, interview with Marcos Vinícius Borges Emmanuel, *O Dia* (27 April 1996)
20. Lima, Roni, 'Advogada pede novo reconhecimento', *Folha de São Paulo* (27 April 1996)
21. Pereira, Robson and Soares, Ronaldo, 'Júri da Candelária começa com confissão', *O Estado de São Paulo* (30 April 96)
22. Tereza, Irany, 'Vagner mantém acusação contra ex-tenente', *O Estado de São Paulo* (30 April 1996)
23. 'Frases', *O Estado de São Paulo* (1 May 1996)

24. Pereira, Robson and Soares, Ronaldo, 'Promotoria lembra outros massacres', *O Estado de São Paulo* (1 May 1996)
25. See 23
26. 'Artista que protegia crianças comemora', *Folha de São Paulo* (1 May 1996)
27. 'Repercussão – julgamento da Candelária', *Folha de São Paulo* (1 May 1996)
28. As above
29. See 23
30. Antunes, Laura, interview with Marcos Vinícius Borges Emmanuel, *O Globo* (2 May 1996)
31. Nunes, Angelina, interview with Nelson Cunha, *O Globo* (4 May 1996)
32. Grillo, Cristina, 'Wagner dos Santos não reconhece o ex-PM que confessou ter atirado nele', *Folha de São Paulo* (1 May 1996)
33. As above
34. As above
35. Torres, Sergio, 'Afirmação de Testemunha será julgada inconsistente', *Folha de São Paulo* (8 May 1996)
36. Rigitano, Cristina, 'Exame liga PM libertado a arma do crime', *Folha de São Paulo* (18 May 1996)
37. As above
38. See 5
39. *Bus 174* (2002), directed by José Padilha
40. *Correio Braziliense* (3 December 2000)
41. See 38
42. De Salgueiro, Helinho and de Souza, Jarbas, lyrics to 'Menino de Pé no Chão', *Neguinho da Beija-FlorAo Vivo,* Trama Promoções Artísticas Ltda

Acknowledgements

My thanks go to the many people whom I interviewed and consulted during the writing of this book. I am particularly indebted to Lúcio Souza Paiva, who first encouraged Wagner to think about writing his story, and whose unpublished account, based on his own interviews with him, kick-started this book; to Dr José Muiños Piñeiro Filho, Andrea Chiesorin and Wagner's sister, Patrícia de Oliveira, for being so generous with their time, contacts and insights; to David Aguiar whose research in Rio's newspaper archives was essential to the completion of the story; to Leonora Klein, Martin Toseland and Tim Cahill for their helpful comments on early drafts; to former DCI David Bright for his entertaining basic introduction to crime-scene investigation; to Clare McMullen and Laura von Mandach for their perspectives on legal aspects of the story; to the Society of Authors for its much-appreciated grant; and to Vision Paperbacks and my agent, Caroline Montgomery, for their enthusiasm for this project.

Most of all, I thank Wagner dos Santos for lending me his life story.